THE SHOOTING SCRIPT

ADAPTATION

THE SHOOTING SCRIPT®

ADAPTATION

SCREENPLAY BY CHARLIE KAUFMAN AND DONALD KAUFMAN

BASED ON THE BOOK "THE ORCHID THIEF," BY SUSAN ORLEAN

FOREWORD BY SUSAN ORLEAN

Q&A WITH CHARLIE KAUFMAN AND SPIKE JONZE

CRITICAL COMMENTARY BY ROBERT McKEE

A Newmarket Shooting Script® Series Book

NEWMARKET PRESS • NEW YORK

FIRST EDITION

9   8   7   6   5

ISBN: 978-1-55704-511-9 (paperback)

10   9   8   7   6   5   4   3   2   1

ISBN: 978-1-55704-580-5 (hardcover)

Library of Congress Catalog-in-Publication Data is available upon request.

QUANTITY PURCHASES

Companies, professional groups, clubs, and other organizations may qualify for special terms when ordering quantities
of this title. For information, write to Special Sales, Newmarket Press, 18 East 48th Street, New York, NY 10017;
call (212) 832-3575 or 1-800-669-3903; FAX (212) 832-3629; or e-mail mailbox@newmarketpress.com.

Website: the United States of America.

OTHER BOOKS IN THE NEWMARKET SHOOTING SCRIPT® SERIES INCLUDE:

OTHER NEWMARKET PICTORIAL MOVIEBOOKS AND NEWMARKET INSIDER FILM BOOKS INCLUDE:

CONTENTS

FOREWORD

BY SUSAN ORLEAN

Let's say you put your beloved child up for adoption, and then let's say the people who come along and scoop the child up are a pair of smart, funny, slightly mad, very imaginative guys who take the child and stretch it every which way, turn it upside down and inside out, dress it up in funny clothes and even change its name, all the while adoring it and doting on it and making sure it ate proper food. A few years later, you are reintroduced to this erstwhile child of yours, who is now quite large and very developed, and certainly not the baby you remembered. This would probably fill you with powerful and peculiar feelings: you do sort of recognize your off-spring, marvel at it, fall freshly in love with it, but definitely understand that it has gone a long way from home.

That is what it's been like for me watching *The Orchid Thief* be transformed into *Adaptation*. It is a strange but perfectly fitting fate for the book. The book's subject—nominally, anyway—is orchids, which happen to be complex organisms that have taken on literally thousands of different forms; they are the most cleverly adaptable living things on earth. In a way, the story of the orchid thief is also a study in shape-shifting. I first stumbled onto the story in 1995. I was flying home from a vacation in Mexico and was looking for something to read. After scouring every page of the Skymall catalogue, I stuck my hand in the seat pocket in front of me and fished around to see if there was anything to look at besides the diagram of the plane's emergency exits.

Susan Orlean has been a staff writer at *The New Yorker* since 1992. It was Orlean's book *The Orchid Thief*, released in January 1999, that brought her to the bestseller lists. Ostensibly the tale of a Florida orchid poacher, Orlean's adventurous and eru-dite journey through the swamps became a riveting look at the nature of obsession and the lengths people will go in the name of passion.

Someone—whoever you are, I owe you—had left a copy of the metro section of that day's *Miami Herald*. Perfect! I love reading metro sections of any newspaper, especially newspapers from cities I don't live in. The *Herald* is a particularly delicious paper to happen upon, since Miami is so full of great metro stories—grisly murders, celebutante misdeeds, weird tropical goings-on. This story was headlined something like, "Local Nurseryman, Seminoles, Arrested in Orchid Poaching," and I read it because I didn't know anything about orchids and didn't know why you would poach one, and I didn't know why a local nurseryman would be partnered up with a group of Seminoles. When I got back to New York, I met with my editor at *The New Yorker* and mentioned the story, and after a few phone calls, headed down to Florida to see what I could see. Once I got there and started reporting, I knew I wanted to go further and expand it into a book.

It was not the easiest book to write. I was far away from home, lonely, hot, and worried. What was the book about? Was it about orchids? Was it the biography of John Laroche, orchid thief? Was it about passion in general? If that were the case, how could you write a book about something abstract like passion? There were times when I was driving across the pancake-flat Florida scrub land in my rental car, when I really wondered what I had gotten myself into. It would be easier to write a genre book—a murder story, a memoir, a crime tale—anything with a conventional narrative arc that followed logical and predictable steps towards climax. Why didn't I do that kind of book? Was it too late to scrap this orchid folly and do something more normal? Every time I was asked what I was working on, I said, "It's a book about this guy….he stole some orchids….but it's about…I can't really exactly say." This kept me awake many nights during the two and a half years I was working on *The Orchid Thief*.

People in Hollywood came calling when the original *New Yorker* story was published in 1995, which came as a great surprise to me, but then again, I am always surprised by what people in Hollywood think. It was such a non-linear, eccentric story that I never imagined someone would picture it as a movie; the orchids would make a nice bit of backdrop, but the story itself seemed too subtle and convoluted for movie-making. As it happens, the book found its way into the hands of Charlie Kaufman, who is a master practitioner of non-linear, eccentric storytelling. When the producers told me—with great excitement—that Charlie had agreed to adapt

The Orchid Thief, I hadn't heard of him; *Being John Malkovich* was not yet released. But the producers were excited, and being an agreeable person, I opted to be excited, too. Why not? By then I had finished the book, felt at peace with it, and was perfectly happy to have someone fool around with it and see if there was a movie inside.

I think I'm lucky: I have had a number of stories optioned for movies and television, and I have the same attitude in every case, which is 1) spell my name right in the credits and 2) give me plenty of notice before the Emmys/Oscars so I can send my dress to the drycleaners in time. I'm not tortured by the thought of someone handling my material. I'm a writer, not a moviemaker. I am not an unrequited screenwriter, director, or actor. Of course, I'd like really wonderful movies to be made from my books because I'd like to go see really wonderful movies. It would be nice to be known as a person who writes stuff that inspires really wonderful movies, but other than that, I don't feel possessive of my stories after that fact. I certainly didn't have a preconceived idea of how I wanted *The Orchid Thief* to be adapted. Privately, I expected someone to do exactly what Charlie protests about in one of the first scenes of *Adaptation*—I assumed it would be made into "an orchid heist movie...or turning it into a movie about drug running...or cramming in sex, or car chases, or guns." I never expected *Adaptation*. But then again, who would?

I didn't meet Charlie until I spent a day on the *Adaptation* set towards the end of the shoot. I was too embarrassed to say much to him, and he seemed too embarrassed to say much to me. What I would have said was that strangely, marvelously, hilariously, his screenplay has ended up not being a literal adaptation of my book, but a spiritual one, something that has captured (and expanded on) the essential character of what the book, I hope, was about: the process of trying to figure out one's self, and life, and love, and the wonders of the world; and the ongoing, exasperating battle between doing what's easy and doing what's good; and the ongoing, exasperating battle between looking at the world ironically and looking at it sentimentally. Oh, and orchids. It is about orchids, about how they adapt to their environment, sometimes resulting in the strangest and most marvelous forms, proving that the answer to everything might indeed be adaptation.

ADAPTATION

Screenplay by Charlie Kaufman and Donald Kaufman

Based on the book "The Orchid Thief" by Susan Orlean

Opening credits are small at the bottom of a black screen. A
male voice plays over them.

                    KAUFMAN (VOICE OVER)
          Do I have an original thought in my head?
          My bald head? Maybe if I were happier,
          my hair wouldn't be falling out. Life is
          short. I need to make the most of it.
          Today is the first day of the rest of my
          life... I'm a walking cliche. I really
          need to go to the doctor and have my leg
          checked. There's something wrong. A
          bump. The dentist called again. I'm way
          overdue. If I stop putting things off, I
          would be happier. All I do is sit on my
          fat ass. If my ass wasn't fat, I would be
          happier. I wouldn't have to wear these
          shirts with the tails out all the time.
          Like that's fooling anyone. Fat-ass! I
          should start jogging again. Five miles a
          day. Really do it this time. Maybe rock
          climbing. I need to turn my life around.
          What do I need to do? I need to fall in
          love. I need to have a girlfriend. I
          need to read more, improve myself. What
          if I learned Russian or something? Or
          took up an instrument? I could speak
          Chinese. I would be the screenwriter who
          speaks Chinese...and plays the oboe.
          That would be cool. I should get my hair
          cut short. Stop trying to fool myself
          and everyone else into thinking I have a
          full head of hair. How pathetic is that?
          Just be real. Confident. Isn't that
          what women are attracted to? Men don't
          have to be attractive. But that's not
          true, especially these days. Almost as
          much pressure on men as there is on women
          these days. Why should I be made to feel
          I have to apologize for my existence?
          Maybe it's my brain chemistry. Maybe
          that's what's wrong with me -- bad
          chemistry. All my problems and anxiety
          can be reduced to a chemical imbalance or
          some kind of misfiring synapses. I need
          to get help for that. But I'll still be
          ugly, though. Nothing's gonna change
          that.

                                             CUT TO:

INT. "BEING JOHN MALKOVICH" SET - DAY

TITLE: ON THE SET OF "BEING JOHN MALKOVICH" SUMMER 1998

It's the "Malkovich Malkovich" restaurant set, but it's
behind-the-scenes footage shot with a hand-held video camera.
The crew is setting up. There are many extras dressed in
rubber over-the-head John Malkovich masks. The actual John
Malkovich sits at one of the tables. He is dressed as a
woman.

                    MALKOVICH
          Shut up! Shut up, okay?

The crew chatter dies down.

                    MALKOVICH (CONT'D)
          Let's really try today to solve our
          camera problems.

TITLE: JOHN MALKOVICH, ACTOR

                    MALKOVICH
          Keep between-take time at an absolute
          minimum. These masks are really hot.
          Okay? I want to be very well heard on
          that from everybody. Don't futz unless
          it's absolutely important to the shot.
          Okay? I don't say that for me. I say
          that for the people sitting here in the
          four hundred pounds of rubber.
               (beat)
          I like my dress. Okay?

The crew laughs. The camera follows the first assistant
director as he walks through the scene.

                    1ST A.D.
          Folks, you better heed that advice.
          Okay? Heed that advice.

TITLE: THOMAS SMITH, FIRST ASSISTANT DIRECTOR

                    1ST A.D.
          Stand by for picture.

The camera follows the first assistant director past the
cinematographer setting up his shot.

                    CINEMATOGRAPHER
          Have her rotate around the table a little
          bit further.

TITLE: LANCE ACORD, CINEMATOGRAPHER

the camera follows the first assistant director to an out-of-the way area where Charlie Kaufman, 40, stands awkwardly by himself.

TITLE: CHARLIE KAUFMAN, SCREENWRITER

> 1ST A.D.
> (to Kaufman)
> You. You're in the eyeline. Can you please get off the stage?

Kaufman exits the soundstage.

EXT. SOUNDSTAGE - CONTINUOUS

Kaufman stands dejectedly outside the soundstage.

> KAUFMAN (VOICE OVER)
> What am I doing here? Why did I bother to come here today? Nobody even seems to know my name. I've been on this planet for forty years, and I'm no closer to understanding a single thing. Why am I here? How did I get here?

EXT. VOLCANIC ERUPTION - DAY

FIRST TITLE: HOLLYWOOD, CALIFORNIA

SECOND TITLE: FOUR BILLION AND FORTY YEARS EARLIER

We move in until we are on the Earth's endlessly barren and lifeless surface. The atmosphere is hazy, toxic-looking. Meteors bombard. Lightning strikes, concussing murky pools of water. All this in silence.

We move in to a murky pool, closer, closer, until we see a single-cell organism multiplying. Soon there are millions of them.

In the ocean: odd, small blind jellyfish collide, recoil, and hover.

A turtle swims, past ancient-looking fish, onto the beach. In the background, leafy plants and small dinosaurs grazing.

Soon we see ancient small mammals, monkeys, ice ages, prehistoric men, cities being built and finally a close-up of a baby being born. As we move into his bawling face,

CUT TO:

INT. L.A. BUSINESS LUNCH RESTAURANT - MIDDAY

Kaufman sitting with Valerie, an attractive woman. They both pick at salads. Kaufman steals glances at her lips, her hair, her breasts. She looks up at him. He blanches, looks down.

> KAUFMAN (VOICE OVER)
> I'm starting to sweat. Stop sweating.
> I've got to stop sweating.

A rivulet of sweat slides down his forehead. Valerie watches it. Kaufman sees her watching it. She sees him seeing her watching it. She looks at her salad. He quickly swabs.

> KAUFMAN (VOICE OVER) (CONT'D)
> Can she see it dripping down my
> forehead?... She looked at my hairline.
> She thinks I'm bald.

> VALERIE
> We think you're great.

> KAUFMAN
> Oh, wow. Thanks. That's nice to hear.

> VALERIE
> We all just loved the "Malkovich" script.

> KAUFMAN
> Thanks. That's....

> VALERIE
> Such a unique voice. Boy, I'd love to
> find a, a portal into your brain.

> KAUFMAN
> (nervous stab at a joke)
> Trust me, it's no fun.

Uncomfortable chuckling from both. Silence.

> VALERIE
> So, tell me your thoughts on this crazy
> little project of ours.

> KAUFMAN
> First, I think it's a great book.

In one motion, Kaufman swabs his forehead and pulls a book entitled The Orchid Thief from his bag.

(CONTINUED)

CONTINUED:

                        VALERIE
            Laroche is a fun character, isn't he?

                        KAUFMAN
            Absolutely. And Orlean makes orchids so
            fascinating. Plus, her, her musings on
            Florida and orchid poaching...

Kaufman flips through the book, stalling. A photo of author
Susan Orlean smiles from the inside back cover.

                        KAUFMAN (CONT'D)
            ...Indians. It's great, sprawling New
            Yorker stuff, and I'd want to remain true
            to that. You know? I'd want to let the
            movie exist, rather than be artificially
            plot driven.

                        VALERIE
            Great.
                (beat)
            I guess I'm not exactly sure what that
            means.

                        KAUFMAN
            Oh. I'm...I'm not sure I know what that
            means, either. Y'know, I just don't want
            to ruin it by making it a Hollywood
            thing. You know? Like an orchid heist
            movie or something, or, y'know, changing
            the orchids into poppies and turning it
            into a movie about drug running, you
            know?

                        VALERIE
            Definitely.

                        KAUFMAN
            Why can't there be a movie simply about
            flowers?

                        VALERIE
            I guess we thought that maybe Susan
            Orlean and Laroche could fall in love,
            and--

                        KAUFMAN
                (blurting)
            Okay. But I'm saying, it's, like, I
            don't want to cram in sex or guns or car
            chases. You know? Or characters
            learning profound life lessons.
                (MORE)

CONTINUED: (2)

> KAUFMAN (CONT'D)
> Or growing, or coming to like each other,
> or overcoming obstacles to succeed in the
> end. You know? I mean, the book isn't
> like that, and life isn't like that. It
> just isn't.
> > (beat, weakly)
> I feel very strongly about this.

Kaufman is sweating like crazy now. Valerie is quiet.

EXT. NEW YORK OFFICE BUILDING - NIGHT

Late night streets. The click-click of typing. We move
slowly up the building to the only glowing window.

TITLE: NEW YORKER MAGAZINE, THREE YEARS EARLIER

INT. OFFICE - CONTINUOUS

We glide over a desk piled with orchid books, past a photo of
Laroche tacked to an overwhelmed bulletin board, and come to
rest on a woman typing. It's Susan Orlean: pale, delicate,
blonde. We lose ourselves in her melancholy beauty.

> ORLEAN (VOICE OVER)
> John Laroche is a tall guy, skinny as a
> stick, pale-eyed, slouch-shouldered,
> sharply handsome, despite the fact he's
> missing all his front teeth. I went to
> Florida two years ago to write a piece
> for The New Yorker. It was after reading
> a small article about a white man and
> three Seminole men arrested with rare
> orchids they'd stolen out of a place
> called the Fakahatchee Strand State
> Preserve.

EXT. STATE ROAD 29 - DAWN

A lonely two-lane highway cutting through swampland.

TITLE: STATE ROAD 29, FLORIDA, TWO YEARS EARLIER

INT. WHITE VAN - CONTINUOUS

John Laroche, a skinny man with no front teeth, drives. The
van is piled with bags of potting soil, gardening junk. A
Writings of Charles Darwin audio cassette case is on the seat
next to Laroche.

(CONTINUED)

CONTINUED:

> BRITISH NARRATOR
> (on tape player)
> As natural selection works solely by and
> for the good of each being, all corporeal
> and mental endowments will tend to
> progress towards perfection... It's
> interesting to contemplate an entangled
> bank, clothed with many kinds...

Laroche tries to contemplate the plants and birds whizzing
by. Almost too late, he spots the Fakahatchee Strand State
Preserve sign and makes a squealing right onto the dirt road
turn-off.

EXT. SWAMP - MORNING

Laroche and three young Indian men, Randy, Russell, and
Matthew, trudge through the waist-high water. Laroche spots
something on a tree and studies it. It's a beautiful small
white orchid.

> LAROCHE
> (awe-struck)
> Polyrrhiza Lindenii. A ghost.
> (suddenly business-like)
> Cut her down, Russell.

As Laroche supervises, the Indians saw through tree branches
supporting lovely flowering orchids. They unceremoniously
stuff the flowers into bulging pillowcases.

INT. RANGER'S TRUCK - MID-MORNING

Tony, a ranger, drives past the Fakahatchee Strand State
Preserve sign and enters the swamp. He sees the parked white
van and an old Ford. He drives past the cars and stops down
the dirt road. He whispers into his C.B.

After a moment, Tony watches through his rear-view mirror as
Laroche steps from the swamp with the Indians, who haul
bulging pillowcases. Tony swerves the truck around and heads
back to the parked cars.

EXT. JANES SCENIC DRIVE - CONTINUOUS

Tony steps out of his truck. Laroche smiles warmly.

> RANGER TONY
> Mornin'.

> LAROCHE
> Hey.

CONTINUED:

                        RANGER TONY
May I ask you gentlemen what you have in
those pillowcases?

                        LAROCHE
Yes, sir, you absolutely may.

                        RANGER TONY
Okay then, I'm askin'.

                        LAROCHE
Well, okay then. Let's see. We got, uh,
five kinds of bromeliad, one peperomia,
nine orchid varieties. Uh, you know
about a hundred and thirty plants all
told. Which my colleagues here removed
from the swamp.

                        RANGER TONY
You are aware it's illegal to remove
plants or animals from state-owned land?

                        LAROCHE
Yeah, and don't forget these plants are
all endangered, sir. Every one of 'em.

                        RANGER TONY
Well, exactly. That's exactly the issue.
This is a state preserve.

                        LAROCHE
Yes, sir. It is.

                        RANGER TONY
But --

                        LAROCHE
Oh, and my colleagues are all Seminole
Indians. Did I mention that? You're
familiar, I'm sure, with the State of
Florida v. James E. Billie. So you know
that even though Seminole Chief Billie
killed a Florida panther, one of...
    (to Indians)
what, forty in the entire world?

                        MATTHEW
Forty.

                        RANDY
Forty.

                                  (CONTINUED)

CONTINUED: (2)

> LAROCHE
> The state couldn't successfully prosecute
> him, 'cause, y'know, he's an Indian, and
> it's his right. As repugnant as you and
> I as white conservationists might find
> his actions.

> RANGER TONY
> But --

> LAROCHE
> Not to mention the failed attempts on
> three separate occasions to prosecute
> Seminoles for poaching palm fronds.
> Which I believe they use to thatch the
> roofs of their traditional chickee huts.
> (to the Indians)
> How 'bout that? Chickee huts, right?

> RUSSELL
> Yeah, he's right. That's exactly what we
> use 'em for. Chickee huts.

> RANDY
> Yeah.

> MATTHEW
> Yeah.

> LAROCHE
> Yeah.

> RANGER TONY
> Yeah, but I don't...Uhh, I can't let
> you fellas leave yet. Just hold on there
> a minute. Okay?

INT. EMPTY HOUSE - DAY

Kaufman enters the house dejectedly. He climbs the stairs.

> DONALD (O.C.)
> Charles, is that you? Did you eat lunch?
> I had that shrimp cocktail in the fridge.
> Was it yours? I hope not. I couldn't
> remember, so I ate it. Maybe we should
> write our names on our food items from
> now on, what do you think?

At the landing Kaufman comes upon Donald, his identical twin
brother, lying on his back on the floor. Kaufman continues
down the hall, barely looking at Donald.

(CONTINUED)

CONTINUED:

                              KAUFMAN
                    What's with you?

                              DONALD
                    My back. Hey, Charles, you'll be glad, I
                    have a plan to get me out of your house,
                    pronto.

                              KAUFMAN
                    A job is a plan. Is your plan a job?

                              DONALD
                    Drumroll, please.
                              (making drumroll sound)
                    I'm gonna be a screenwriter! Like you!
                    Okay, I know you think this is just one
                    of my get-rich-quick schemes, but I'm
                    doing it right this time. I'm taking a
                    three-day seminar.

Kaufman doesn't respond, enters his bedroom.

INT. EMPTY BEDROOM - CONTINUOUS

Kaufman lies face down on his mattress on the floor.

                              DONALD (O.S)
                    And it's only five hundred bucks!

Kaufman pulls a photo of Amelia, 30's, clipped out of a
newsletter, from under his pillow. He gets lost in the
picture.

NEWSPAPER CAPTION READS: Violinist Amelia Kavan in our
ongoing series of local recitals, we present Ms. Kavan
performing Beethoven's Opus 51 for her Pasadena Community
Center debut.

                              KAUFMAN
                    Screenwriting seminars are bullshit.

                              DONALD (O.S.)
                    In theory I agree with you. But this
                    one's different. This one's highly
                    regarded in the industry.

                              KAUFMAN
                    Donald, don't say "industry".

                              DONALD (O.S.)
                    I'm sorry, I forgot. Charles, this guy
                    knows screenwriting.

                                                    (CONTINUED)

CONTINUED:

Donald appears on all fours in the doorway. Kaufman puts the
photo back under his pillow.

> DONALD (CONT'D)
> People come from all over to study with
> him. I'll pay you back, buddy, just as
> soon as I sell the --

> KAUFMAN
> Let me explain something to you.

> DONALD
> Okay.

> KAUFMAN
> Anybody who says he's got "the answer" is
> going to attract desperate people, be it
> in the world of religion--

> DONALD
> I just need to lie down while you explain
> this to me. Sorry. I apologize. Okay,
> go ahead.

> KAUFMAN
> So --

> DONALD
> (adjusting himself)
> Sorry. Okay. Go.

> KAUFMAN
> There are no rules, Donald, and anybody
> who says there are, is just --

> DONALD
> Oh, wait. Not rules. Principles. McKee
> writes that a rule says you must do it
> this way. A principle says this works
> and has through all remembered time.

> KAUFMAN
> The script I'm starting, it's about
> flowers.

> DONALD
> Ohhhh!

> KAUFMAN
> Nobody's ever done a movie about flowers
> before. So there are no guidelines.

(CONTINUED)

CONTINUED: (2)

                    DONALD
          What about <u>Flowers for Algernon</u>?

                    KAUFMAN
          Well no, that's not about flowers.

                    DONALD
          Oh, oh, okay.

                    KAUFMAN
          And it's not a movie.

                    DONALD
          I'm sorry, I never saw it. Okay, keep
          going.

                    KAUFMAN
          Look, my point is that those teachers are
          dangerous if your goal is to try to do
          something new. And a writer should
          always have that goal. Writing is a
          journey into the unknown. It's not...
          building one of your model airplanes!

Both brothers stare at the ceiling. Donald finally speaks

                    DONALD
          McKee is a former Fulbright scholar,
          Charles. Are you a former Fulbright
          scholar?

INT. APARTMENT BUILDING HALLWAY - CONTINUOUS

There's a party spilling out from an apartment. Kaufman sits
down the hall, on the floor with Amelia. They drink wine
from plastic cups and are both tipsy. Amelia looks out the
window at the city lights.

                    KAUFMAN (VOICE OVER)
          I should say something. I need to say
          something funny, or something smart, or
          sensitive. Think.

                    KAUFMAN (CONT'D)
          I hate parties, Amelia. Why did we come
          here?

Amelia looks over at the partygoers in the hall.

                    AMELIA
          Because we're hip young trendsetters on
          the make? Aren't we?

                                        (CONTINUED)

CONTINUED:

                         KAUFMAN
          More like old losers on the floor.

                         AMELIA
          Jesus, Charlie. Speak for
          yourself.

Kaufman chuckles, embarrassed. Amelia studies him

                         AMELIA (CONT'D)
          Okay. Charlie, we're gonna fix you up.
          We're gonna solve the whole Charlie
          Kaufman mess once and for all.

                         KAUFMAN
               (nervous but pleased)
          Okay.

                         AMELIA
          Okay, let me see. What do you need?
          What, what, what?
               (thinks)
          Well, I'm glad you took the orchid
          script.

                         KAUFMAN
          Yeah?

                         AMELIA
          Yeah. I think it will be good for you to
          get out of your head. I think it'll
          ground you to think about the bigger
          picture, about nature and stuff.

                         KAUFMAN
          I still can't believe they gave me that
          job. I mean, after that lunch. I was
          sweating insanely. I was ranting.

                         AMELIA
          Oh, you were just nervous 'cause she was
          pretty, that's all.

                         KAUFMAN
          How do you know she was pretty?

                         AMELIA
          After eight months of knowing you, I
          think I get what makes you sweat.

                         KAUFMAN
          Okay, okay.

                                        (CONTINUED)

CONTINUED: (2)

>   AMELIA
>   Well, whatever. Moving on, what next?
>   Oh, you need a new get-up. This whole
>   flannel shirt thing, it's not really
>   doing anything for you anymore.

Kaufman laughs. Amelia joins in. Pause.

>   KAUFMAN
>   Thanks for coming out with me tonight,
>   Amelia.

They look at each other. It's a kiss moment. Nothing
happens. The moment passes. Kaufman is embarrassed. Amelia
seems sad. There is a long pause. Kaufman sips his wine,
his hand shaking a little.

INT. EMPTY BEDROOM & VARIOUS

Kaufman in front of typewriter, ready to write.

>   KAUFMAN
>   To begin. To begin. How to start. I'm
>   hungry. I should get coffee. Coffee
>   would help me think. But I should write
>   something first. Then reward myself with
>   coffee. Coffee and a muffin. Okay, so I
>   need to establish the themes.
>   (pause)
>   Maybe banana nut. That's a good muffin.

INT. ORLEAN'S APARTMENT - NIGHT

Orlean types. Her delicate fingers move with a pianist's
grace across the computer keyboard

>   ORLEAN (VOICE OVER)
>   Orchid hunting is a mortal occupation.

EXT. TROPICAL RIVER - DAY

TITLE: ORINOCO RIVER, ONE HUNDRED YEARS EARLIER

An overturned boat and uprooted orchids float on the river.

>   ORLEAN (VOICE OVER)
>   The Victorian-era orchid hunter William
>   Arnold drowned on a collecting
>   expedition.

EXT. RIVER - NIGHT

TITLE: KINABALU, BORNEO

a lone boot on a log in a pond.

>   ORLEAN (VOICE OVER)
>   Osmers vanished without a trace in Asia.

                                                    CUT TO:

EXT. RIVER - NIGHT

TITLE: XISHUANGBANNA, CHINA

An emaciated, limping, wheezing man with a makeshift bandage
wrapped around his head, docks his boat.

>   ORLEAN (VOICE OVER)
>   Augustus Margary survived toothache,
>   rheumatism, pleurisy and dysentery only
>   to be murdered when he completed his
>   mission and traveled beyond Bhamo.

Someone steps from behind a bush, stabs him, steals his boat.
The murderer sails down river.

EXT. SWAMP - LATE MORNING

Ranger, sheriff, and state police cars are parked near the
van and Ford. Lots of sweating, uniformed people. The
pillowcases have been emptied, the plants lie on black
plastic sheets. A guy sprinkles water on them. Laroche
enthusiastically helps Ranger Steve Neely catalogue the
flowers. The Indians lean against their car, bored and
smoking. Nirvana seeps tinnily out the car window.

>   ORLEAN (VOICE OVER)
>   Laroche loved orchids, but I came to
>   believe he loved the difficulty and
>   fatality of getting them almost as much
>   as he loved the orchids themselves.

INT. COURT ROOM - DAY

The proceedings are in progress. Orlean hurries in, sits in
the back. Laroche, in a Miami Hurricanes cap, wrap-around
Mylar sunglasses, and a Hawaiian shirt, is on the stand.
Alan Lerner, the tribe's lawyer, questions him.

>   LAROCHE
>   I've been a professional horticulturist
>   for, like, twelve years. I own my own
>   plant nursery, which was destroyed by the
>   hurricane.
>   (MORE)

                                              (CONTINUED)

CONTINUED:

                    LAROCHE (CONT'D)
          I'm a professional plant lecturer. I've
          given over, like, sixty lectures on the
          cultivation of plants. I'm a published
          author, both in magazine and book form.
          And I have extensive experience with
          orchids and the asexual
          micropropagation of orchids under aseptic
          cultures. And it's laboratory work.
          Y'know, it's not at all like your nursery
          work.
                    (chuckles)
          I'm probably the smartest person I know.

                    LERNER
          Thank you.

                    LAROCHE
          You're very welcome.

EXT. COURTHOUSE - DAY

Orlean exits the courthouse and watches Laroche in a huddle
with Lerner, Matthew, and Buster Baxley, vice-president of
the tribe's business operations. They're all smoking
intently.

Lerner starts to protest something; Buster waves a dismissive
hand, walks away. Matthew shrugs, stubs his cigarette,
follows Buster. Lerner and Laroche stand there a moment
silently. Lerner walks off. Laroche cracks his neck. A
charmingly shy Orlean approaches.

                    ORLEAN
          Mister Laroche? I'm Susan Orlean. I'm a
          writer for The New Yorker. It's a
          magazine that--

                    LAROCHE
          I'm familiar with The New Yorker. *The
          New Yorker, yes, The New Yorker*. Right?

                    ORLEAN
                    (laughing)
          Yes, that, that's right. Um, I'm very
          interested in doing a piece on, on your
          situation down here, and I was just --

                    LAROCHE
          Oh, yeah? Put this in. I don't care
          what goes on here. I'm right...and I'll
          take it all the way to the Supreme Court.
          That judge can go screw herself.

                                        (CONTINUED)

CONTINUED:

Orlean scribbles on her pad. Laroche twists his head to see
what she's writing.

>   LAROCHE (CONT'D)
>   That for real would go in?

>   ORLEAN
>   Absolutely.

Laroche smiles his toothless smile at Orlean.

INT. EMPTY BEDROOM - DAY

Kaufman traces a stubby, nail-bitten finger along State Road
29 on a Florida road map. He turns to his typewriter, and
types in a clumsy hunt-and-peck style.

>   KAUFMAN (VOICE OVER)
>   We open on State Road twenty-nine. A
>   battered white van speeds along making a
>   sharp skidding right into the Fakahatchee
>   Strand State Preserve. The driver of the
>   van is a skinny man with no front teeth.
>   This is John Laroche.

Kaufman stops, sits there.

>   KAUFMAN (CONT'D)
>   I need a break.

INT. KAUFMAN'S CAR - NIGHT

Kaufman drives. Amelia is in the front passenger seat. Both
are dressed in concert-going clothes. Both seem nervous.
There's a silence, then:

>   AMELIA
>   I really loved the Sibelius violin
>   concerto.

>   KAUFMAN
>   Yeah, me, too. It was great. The end
>   was a little weird, though. But --

>   AMELIA
>   Oh, no, God, it was passionate. It was
>   exultant. The soloist was amazing! Such
>   beautiful tones. So precise. Oh, God,
>   it blows my mind. Oh, I wish I could
>   play like that.

>   KAUFMAN
>   You do!

CONTINUED:

                         AMELIA
             Charlie. I don't. I'm mediocre at best.

                         KAUFMAN
             What? I love listening to you play.

                         AMELIA
             Thanks, Charlie.
                  (chuckles)
             Well...here we are.

Another silence. Kaufman pulls to the curb, parks. Beat.

                         AMELIA (CONT'D)
             So, what are you up to now, then?

                         KAUFMAN
             Oh, um, I should probably get to bed. I
             have a lot of work to do tomorrow.

                         AMELIA
             Well, good night, then.

Another silence.

                         KAUFMAN
             I would stay out -- It's just that I've
             really been struggling with the script.
             I've been thinking about it too small.
             Just writing it like a story about
             Laroche. That's not enough. I mean, I
             wanted to write about flowers. Anyway, I
             can't figure it out, and I haven't been
             sleeping very well lately, so I thought I
             should get home and try to get a good
             night's sleep, y'know? Start fresh in
             the morning.

                         AMELIA
             Mm.

                         KAUFMAN
             Otherwise, I'd stay out.

                         AMELIA
             I understand. I hope you figure it out,
             Charlie. I really do.

                         KAUFMAN
             Thanks. Thanks for coming out with me
             and everything.

(CONTINUED)

CONTINUED: (2)

                    AMELIA
          Sure, it was fun.

                    KAUFMAN
          So, um, anyway... I have to go to Santa
          Barbara next weekend for this orchid show
          up there. I thought maybe you could
          come.

                    AMELIA
          No, I don't think I can make it next
          weekend. I don't think I can. I've got
          something. Sorry.

                    KAUFMAN
          Okay. So, well, okay, then, so, good
          night, then.

                    AMELIA
          Good night, Charlie.

She closes the car door and heads to her house. Kaufman
watches as she opens the front door, enters the house, and
closes the door. She doesn't look back.

                    KAUFMAN (VOICE OVER)
          Why didn't I go in? I'm such a chicken.
          I'm such an idiot. I should have kissed
          her. I've blown it. I should just go
          and knock on her door right now and kiss
          her. It would be romantic. Something we
          could someday tell our kids. I'm gonna
          do that right now.

Kaufman drives away.

EXT. HOTEL PARKING LOT - MORNING

Orlean leans against a car and smokes. A tiny, lost figure.
There's a honk. Orlean snaps out of her reverie to see
Laroche screeching to a stop in his banged-up van.

TITLE: FLORIDA, THREE YEARS EARLIER

                    ORLEAN
          Thanks for picking me up.

She opens the passenger door.

                    LAROCHE
          Yeah, I want you to know this van's a
          piece of shit, but when I hit the
          jackpot, I'll buy myself an awesome car.
                    (MORE)

                                              (CONTINUED)

CONTINUED:

>   LAROCHE (CONT'D)
>   (thought)
>   Hey, what are you driving?
>
>
>   ORLEAN
>   Um...it's, well, it's a rental. It's a
>   Lumina.
>
>   LAROCHE
>   Awesome. I think I'll get one of those,
>   too.

Orlean nods, climbs in, and tries to rearrange some of the
junk on the front seat so she'll have a place to sit. She
situates herself on the edge of the seat, rests her feet on
an open bag of potting soil. Laroche lurches off.

INT. VAN - DAY

Laroche drives manically. Orlean watches the road and holds
a hand against the dashboard.

>   LAROCHE
>   Where do these people learn to drive?
>   (laughs)
>   The world's insane.

Orlean switches on a mini-cassette recorder, pulls out a
notebook. Laroche clams up. Orlean tries to figure a way
in.

>   ORLEAN
>   So I was impressed to hear how
>   accomplished you are in the world of
>   horticulture.
>
>   LAROCHE
>   Yeah, yeah, look. The thing you gotta
>   know is my whole life is looking for a
>   goddamn profitable plant, see? And
>   that's the ghost.
>
>   ORLEAN
>   Mm-hm. Why the ghost orchid?

ORLEAN WRITES IN NOTEPAD: piles of crap. funny smell in van.

>   LAROCHE
>   Well the sucker's rare. Y'know? And I'm
>   the only one in the world who knows how
>   to cultivate it. See, the idea was, get
>   the Indians to pull it from the swamp.
>   'Cause I researched it. Long as I don't
>   touch the plant, Florida can't touch us.
>   (MORE)

CONTINUED:

LAROCHE (CONT'D)
And I stop future poaching by makin' the
flowers readily available in stores. I'm
a hero, the flowers are saved -- Laroche
and nature win!

ORLEAN WRITES IN NOTEPAD: delusions of grandeur.

LAROCHE (CONT'D)
Did you get that last part?

ORLEAN
Yeah, I sure did.

INT. EMPTY DINING ROOM - A BIT LATER

Kaufman sits at a card table in the otherwise empty room. He
picks at his salad and reads Orlean's book. Donald lies on
the floor, chomping a hoagie and reading a copy of Story by
Robert Mckee.

ORLEAN (VOICE OVER)
Orchids are the sexiest flowers on Earth.
The name "orchid" derives from the Latin
orchis, which means testicle.

DONALD
Hey, Charles. I pitched mom my
screenplay.

KAUFMAN
Don't say "pitch".

DONALD
Sorry. Anyway, she said it was "Silence
of the Lambs" meets "Psycho."

KAUFMAN
Yeah, well, maybe you guys could
collaborate. I hear mom's really good
with structure.

DONALD
(beat, then pissy)
So, how come Amelia doesn't come around
anymore? Did you put the moves on her or
something?

Kaufman looks over at Donald, who smiles at him, cheeks
stuffed with food.

EXT. SEMINOLE NURSERY - DAY

Orlean pulls up to the nursery. A few Indians are hauling
plants. She recognizes Matthew from the courthouse.

(CONTINUED)

CONTINUED:

Today he's wearing a green t-shirt with white skulls. His
long-black hair is braided. He's handsome. Orlean
approaches.

> ORLEAN
> Hi! I'm looking for John Laroche.
> I'm writing an article on John, and I
> just stopped by. I hoped I could see
> him.

Matthew comes over to her. His eyes are gentle. She's
taken.

> MATTHEW
> John's not here today.

> ORLEAN
> Oh. Well, you were at the swamp with
> him, weren't you? I saw you at the
> courthouse is how I know.

> MATTHEW
> Yes. I'm Matthew Osceola.

> ORLEAN
> Susan Orlean. Nice to meet you. Maybe I
> could talk to you for a second? I'm just
> trying to get a little feel for --

> MATTHEW
> You have very beautiful hair.

He gently reaches out and touches it.

> ORLEAN
> Oh, thank you very much. I just, um, I
> just washed it this morning. I used a
> new conditioner.

> MATTHEW
> I can see your sadness. It's lovely.

> ORLEAN
> Well, I'm --
>   (laughing)
> -- just tired, that's all. That's my
> problem. So maybe we could chat a little
> bit, and y'know, I could get some
> background for --

> MATTHEW
> I'm not going to talk to you much. It's
> not personal. It's the Indian way.

(CONTINUED)

CONTINUED: (2)

He touches her hand and heads back to work. She watches him haul potted plants, immersed in the activity, muscles straining against his shirt. She just stands there.

INT. SHOW HALL - DAY

Crowded with orchid lovers. Orlean and Laroche walk among them. Laroche spots an orchid.

> LAROCHE
> *Angraecum sesquipedale*. Beauty! God!
> Darwin wrote about this one...

Laroche runs over to a flower, fondles its petals.

> LAROCHE (CONT'D)
> ...Charles Darwin? Evolution guy?
> Hello?

> ORLEAN
> Mm.

> LAROCHE
> You see that nectary all the way down
> there? Darwin hypothesized a moth with a
> nose twelve inches long to pollinate it.
> Everyone thought he was a loon. Then,
> sure enough, they found this moth with a
> twelve-inch proboscis. Proboscis means
> nose by the way.

> ORLEAN
> I know what proboscis means.

> LAROCHE
> Hey, let's not get off the subject. This
> isn't a pissing contest. The point is,
> what's so wonderful is that every one of
> these flowers has a specific relationship
> with the insect that pollinates it.
> There's a certain...

EXT. MEADOW - DAY

We're with an insect as it buzzes along.

> LAROCHE (VOICE OVER)
> ...orchid looks exactly like a certain
> insect, so the...insect is drawn to this
> flower. Its double. Its soul mate. And
> wants nothing more than to make love to
> it.
> (MORE)

(CONTINUED)

CONTINUED:

                    LAROCHE (VOICE OVER) (CONT'D)
      After the insect flies off, it spots
      another soul mate flower and makes love
      to it, thus pollinating it. And neither
      the flower nor the insect will ever
      understand the significance of their
      lovemaking. I mean, how could they know
      that because of their little dance the
      world lives? But it does. By simply
      doing what they're designed to do,
      something large and magnificent happens.
      In this sense, they show us how to live.
      How the...

The insect, covered in pollen, flies away. It joins
thousands of insects doing the same thing: flying, buzzing
around flowers.

INT. SHOW HALL - DAY

Orlean looks at Laroche. In the background people buzz
around flowers: feel petals, stare deep into nectaries,
jabber passionately, carry boxes of plants.

                    LAROCHE
      ...only barometer you have is your heart.
      How when you spot your flower, you can't
      let anything get in your way.

Orlean looks at Laroche, then deeply into various flowers: a
dizzying array of colors and shapes.

INT. APARTMENT - EARLY EVENING

Orlean sits at the dining room table with her husband and
three other couples. Smart New York folks.

                    HUSBAND
      He's really quite a character. No front
      teeth. Doesn't seem to bother him at all
      though.

                    FEMALE GUEST #1
      Why doesn't he get them fixed? It seems
      almost sociopathic to make everybody look
      at that.

                    MALE GUEST #2
      Bet he gives a great blow job, honey.

Orlean laughs. Dinner guests laugh, groan, and mutter.

                    ORLEAN
      He is a fascinating character, though.

CONTINUED:

                      FEMALE GUEST #1
Sounds like a goldmine, Sue.

                      ORLEAN
Oh, it could be. I don't know, y'know?
He lives with his dad, he's obsessed with
his dead mother, and, oh, he wears his
sunglasses on a little dingle-dangle
around his neck.

                      MALE GUEST #2
I love it.

                      HUSBAND
Tell them about the van.

                      ORLEAN
Okay, the van. The van. I can't tell
about the van, I gotta pee.

                      MALE GUEST #2
You did it in the van.

Dinner guests laugh.

                      ORLEAN
        (to Guest #2)
Shut up!
        (to Husband)
David, you tell-- Don't you tell them.
Don't tell them about the van.

                      HUSBAND
Okay.
        (to guests)
The van...

Dinner guests laugh.

                      ORLEAN
        (shouting)
David!

We follow the giggling Orlean into the bathroom as her
husband talks.

                      HUSBAND
The van was filled with junk.

                      ORLEAN
Shut up!

INT. BATHROOM - CONTINUOUS

Orlean closes the door behind her. As she passes the mirror,
she briefly catches the shit-eating grin on her face. She
leans against the door and hears the muffled conversation and
laughter in the dining room.

> HUSBAND (O.S.)
> Potting soil, pebbles, food wrappers,
> fertilizer.

ORLEAN takes a breath.

> HUSBAND (O.S.) (CONT'D)
> Susie said she hoped it was fertilizer,
> anyway. She said she couldn't be sure,
> that Laroche had a certain aromatic look
> about him.

She looks quickly away, ashamed. The smile's gone. Dinner
guests laugh off-screen.

> HUSBAND (O.S) (CONT'D)
> And she said, perhaps his obsessiveness
> didn't leave room in his schedule for
> personal hygiene. Or that maybe the
> orchids got all the available water.

> ORLEAN (VOICE OVER)
> (staring at reflection)
> I wanted to want something as much as
> people wanted...

INT. APARTMENT - LATER

Orlean is back at the dining room table. The joking
conversation is going on. She is participating but with no
enthusiasm. She has been crying.

> ORLEAN (VOICE OVER)
> ...these plants. But it isn't part of my
> constitution. I suppose I do have one
> unembarrassed passion...

INT. BEDROOM - LATER

Orlean lies in bed with her husband. He sleeps. She stares
up at the ceiling.

> ORLEAN (VOICE OVER)
> ...I want to know what it feels like to
> care about something passionately.

INT. NEW YORKER OFFICE - EVENING

Orlean looks at a book called <u>The Native Orchids of Florida</u>.
She sees a photo of a ghost orchid glowing white on the page.
A line of text catches her eye: "Should one be lucky enough
to see a flower all else will seem eclipsed." Orlean closes
the book, sits there. She dials the phone.

                    ORLEAN (VOICE OVER)
               If the ghost orchid was really a
               phantom...

EXT. FIELD - MORNING

MUSIC: lush, profound orchestral piece.

A glorious orange, large-petalled orchid blooms in dramatic
time-lapse. We slowly, lovingly circle the flower.

                    ORLEAN (VOICE OVER)
               ...it was still such a bewitching one
               that it could seduce people to pursue it
               year after year and mile after miserable
               mile. If it was a real flower, I wanted
               to see one. The reason was not that I
               love orchids. I don't even especially
               like orchids. What I wanted was to see
               this thing...that people were drawn to in
               such a singular and powerful way.

INT. VAN - DAY

Laroche drives. Orlean studies him for a moment, her sad
eyes wet and glistening. The tape recorder is on between
them.

                    ORLEAN (VOICE OVER)
               So... how many turtles did you end up
               collecting?

                    LAROCHE
               Oh, I lost interest right after that.

                    ORLEAN
                    (confused)
               Oh.

                    LAROCHE
               I dropped turtles when I fell in love
               with Ice Age fossils. Collected the shit
               out of 'em. I mean, fossils were the only
               thing that made sense to me in this
               fucked-up world.
                    (MORE)

(CONTINUED)

CONTINUED:

                          LAROCHE (CONT'D)
I ditched fossils for resilvering old
mirrors. My mom and I had the largest
collection of nineteenth century Dutch
mirrors on the planet. Perhaps you read
about us. Mirror World, October eighty-
eight? I got a copy here somewhere.

Laroche fishes through junk as he drives.

                          ORLEAN
I guess I'd just like to know how you can
detach from something that you've
invested so much of your soul in. I
mean, didn't you ever miss turtles...
     (reading from notepad)
...The only thing that made your ten-year-
old life worth living?

                          LAROCHE
Look, I'll tell you a story. All right?
I once fell deeply, you know, profoundly
in love with tropical fish. I had sixty
goddamn fish tanks in my house. I'd skin
dive to find just the right ones.
Anisotremus virginicus, *Holacanthus
ciliaris*, *Chaetodon capistratus*. You
name it. Then one day I say, fuck fish.
I renounce fish. I vow never to set foot
in that ocean again. That's how much
"fuck fish". That was seventeen years
ago, and I have never since stuck so much
as a toe in that ocean. And I love the
ocean!

                          ORLEAN
But why?

                          LAROCHE
Done with fish.

                       ORLEAN (VOICE OVER)
If you'd really loved something wouldn't
a little bit of it linger? Evidently
Laroche's finishes were downright and
absolute. He just moved on....

INT. L.A. PASTA PLACE - DAY

Kaufman, in a booth, reads The Orchid Thief, takes notes.

                     ORLEAN (VOICE OVER)
...I sometimes wished I could do the
same.

                                     (CONTINUED)

CONTINUED:

KAUFMAN sighs, looks up, watches a waitress with glorious,
orange hair, pouty lips, soulful eyes, and a voluptuous form,
turning slowly around, scanning her station. She sees
Kaufman, approaches, smiles warmly down at him. Her badge
reads: Alice, Arcadia, CA. Kaufman sweats.

                    ALICE
          Good afternoon. So, what looks good
          today?

                    KAUFMAN
          Uh, the key lime pie, please. A small
          slice. And, and a coffee, please. Skim
          milk, please.

Alice spots The Orchid Thief on the table.

                    ALICE
          Orchids! I love orchids.

                    KAUFMAN
               (gone blank)
          Cool. That's....

He flinches at his lameness. An awkward pause.

                    ALICE
          Well, I'll be right back with your pie.

She smiles warmly again and leaves. Kaufman is humiliated.

EXT. ORCHID SHOW - DAY

Alice, in her uniform, and Kaufman walk hand-in-hand,
inspecting sexy orchids together. They stop to look at one
beautiful flower.

                    ALICE
          I'm so excited. I've always wanted to
          come to an orchid show. I think these
          flowers are so sexy.

Alice stands very close to Kaufman. Her bare arm touches
his. Kaufman looks at the touching arms. Alice continues to
study the flower but intertwines her fingers in Kaufman's.

                    ALICE (CONT'D)
          Let's see what's around back.

EXT. WOODED AREA - DAY

She leads Kaufman behind the display to a quiet, wooded area.
She unbuttons her uniform.

                                        (CONTINUED)

CONTINUED:

It falls to the ground, leaving her naked, dappled in
sunlight, her beautiful red hair glowing. Kaufman drops to
his knees in front of her and kisses her thighs, caresses her
ass. Alice guides Kaufman's head to her crotch. There's a
knocking sound.

INT. EMPTY BEDROOM - NIGHT

Kaufman, in bed masturbating, looks up at the closed door.

                    KAUFMAN
          What?!

The door opens. Donald stands there for a moment in shadows.

                    DONALD
          You wanna hear my pitch?

                    KAUFMAN
          Go away, goddamn it!

                    DONALD
              (beat, lost)
          You know, I'm just trying to do
          something...

Kaufman squints at his brother, sits up, waits.

                    DONALD (CONT'D)
          ...Hey, thanks a lot, buddy.
          Cool...Okay, there's this serial killer,
          right?

Kaufman groans, lies back down, stares at the ceiling.

                    DONALD (CONT'D)
          No wait! And he's being hunted by a cop.
          And he's taunting the cop, right?
          Sending clues who his next victim is.
          He's already holding her hostage in his
          creepy basement. So the cop gets
          obsessed with figuring out her identity,
          and in the process falls in love with
          her. Even though he's never even met
          her. She becomes like the unattainable.
          Like the Holy Grail.

                    KAUFMAN
          It's a little obvious, don't you think?

                    DONALD
          Okay, but here's the twist. We find out
          that the killer really suffers from
          multiple personality disorder. Right?
              (MORE)

                                        (CONTINUED)

CONTINUED:

                    DONALD (CONT'D)
See, he's actually really the cop *and* the
girl. All of them are him! Isn't that
fucked up?!

Donald waits, proud. Kaufman stares up at the ceiling.

                    KAUFMAN
The only idea more overused than serial
killers is multiple personality. On top
of that, you explore the notion that cop
and criminal are really two aspects of
the same person. See every cop movie
ever made for other examples of this.

                    DONALD
Mom called it psychologically taut.

                    KAUFMAN
The other thing is, there's no way to
write this. Did you consider that? I
mean, how could you have somebody held
prisoner in a basement and working in a
police station at the same time?

                    DONALD
Trick photography?

                    KAUFMAN
Okay, that's not what I'm asking. Listen
closely. What I'm asking is, in the
reality of this movie, where there's only
one character, right? Okay? How could
you.... What, what exactly would....

Donald waits blankly. Kaufman gives up, gets out of bed.

                    KAUFMAN (CONT'D)
I agree with Mom. Very taut. "Sybil"
meets, I don't know..."Dressed to Kill".

                    DONALD
Cool. I really liked "Dressed to Kill".
Until the third act denouement.

                    KAUFMAN
That's not how it's pronounced.

                    DONALD
Sorry. I, I-- Okay, sorry.

Kaufman dresses and exits.

INT. L.A. PASTA PLACE - DAY

Kaufman, hair combed, sits nervously in a booth, watching
Alice. He tenses as she approaches. She smiles warmly.

                    KAUFMAN
          Hi.

                    ALICE
          Hey! Some key lime pie for you today?

                    KAUFMAN
          Okay, yeah. That sounds great.

                    ALICE
          I'll cut you an extra large slice.
          Preferred customer.

She winks at him. He's so in love.

                    KAUFMAN
          Thank you. That's really sweet of you.

                    ALICE
          Well, I'm just a sweetie, ain't I?
               (giggles)
          Still reading about orchids, I hope?

                    KAUFMAN
          Yes, I am.

                    ALICE
          This friend of mine has this little tiny
          pink one that grows on a tree branch,
          just like that. I can't remember what --

                    KAUFMAN
          That's what's called an epiphyte.

                    ALICE
          Right! Right! Boy, you know your stuff.

                    KAUFMAN
          No not really. I'm just learning.
          Epiphytes grow on trees, but they're not
          parasites. They get all their
          nourishment from the air and the rain.

                    ALICE
          Well, I'm impressed. That's great.

                                        (CONTINUED)

CONTINUED:

                      KAUFMAN
       There are more than thirty thousand kinds
       of orchids in the world.

                      ALICE
       Wow, that's a lot, huh?

                      KAUFMAN
       Yeah.

Awkward silence.

                      ALICE
       So.... I'll be right back with an extra
       large slice of key lime pie for my orchid
       expert.

He beams. She smiles and turns to leave. Kaufman blurts:

                      KAUFMAN
       But, so anyway, I was also wondering...?

Alice turns back, still smiling.

                  KAUFMAN (CONT'D)
       ...I'm going up to Santa Barbara this
       Saturday for an orchid show and I, and I--
       I...

Alice's smile slips away. Her warmth dissipates.

                      ALICE
       Oh.

                      KAUFMAN
       I'm sorry. I apologize.

                      ALICE
       So I'll just --

                      KAUFMAN
       I'm sorry.

                      ALICE
       -- be right back with your pie then.

He nods, watches Alice walk away and say something to another
waitress. The other waitress looks over at him.

EXT. SANTA BARBARA ORCHID SHOW - DAY

Kaufman walks alone among the crowd of orchid enthusiasts,
past a Santa Barbara Orchid Society sign. He tries to study
the flowers. They are dull. He forces himself to look.

> ORLEAN (VOICE OVER)
> There are more than thirty thousand known
> orchid species. One looks like a turtle.
> One looks like a monkey. One looks like
> an onion. One looks like a German
> Shepherd. One looks like...

Kaufman finds his attention drifting from orchids to women:
all different shapes, colors, personalities, some in subtle
clothing, some in garish clothing, all glowing.

> KAUFMAN (VOICE OVER)
> ...a schoolteacher...One looks like a
> gymnast. One looks like that girl in high
> school with creamy skin. One looks like
> a New York intellectual with whom you do
> the Sunday Times crossword puzzle in bed.
> One looks like a midwestern beauty queen.
> One looks like Amelia. One has eyes that
> dance. One has eyes...

He is sick with adoration for the women, who pay him no mind.

INT. ORLEAN'S APARTMENT - NIGHT

Orlean types.

> KAUFMAN (VOICE OVER)
> ...that contain the sadness of the world.

It's pouring and sheets of rain beat against her window. She
glances at her husband, across the room reading a book.

INT. VAN - NIGHT

Laroche drives. Orlean looks out at the dark night.

> LAROCHE
> So I got married, and me and my beautiful
> new wife, my now ex-wife, the bitch,
> opened up a nursery. People started
> coming out of the woodwork to ask me
> stuff and...admire my plants and admire
> me. I think some people were really
> spending time with me because they were
> lonely.

(CONTINUED)

CONTINUED:

Orlean reacts to this. She feels caught.

                    LAROCHE (CONT'D)
          You know why I like plants?

                    ORLEAN
          Huh-uh.

                    LAROCHE
          'Cause they're so mutable...Adaptation's
          a profound process. It means you figure
          out how to thrive in the world.

Orlean looks at him. After a long silence:

                    ORLEAN
          Yeah, but it's easier for plants. I
          mean, they have no memory, y'know. They
          just move on to whatever's next. But for
          a person adapting is almost shameful.
          It's like running away.

INT. 7 1/2 FLOOR SET - MORNING

The set from Being John Malkovich. Crew people bustle about,
bending down as they enter the squat set. No one pays any
attention to Kaufman, who stands by himself to the side.

John Cusack passes Kaufman. Kaufman waves. Cusack nods
perfunctorily.

Donald is at the craft service table, picking at food.
Caroline, a pretty, young make-up woman, stops by the table.
Kaufman watches nervously as Donald eyes her. Finally Donald
says something to her. She looks over, says something back.
It's too far away to hear the conversation. Donald says
something else and Caroline laughs. The conversation warms
up. Kaufman can't believe his eyes. Catherine Keener heads
toward the set and Caroline joins her. The two pass Kaufman.
Kaufman waves. Keener eyes him suspiciously.

Donald approaches Kaufman.

                    DONALD
          Hey, man.

                    KAUFMAN
          Please don't hit on crew members, Donald.

                    DONALD
          What? The makeup girl? She was hitting
          on me, bro.

                                              (CONTINUED)

CONTINUED:

                    KAUFMAN
          Just don't embarrass me, okay? I have to
          work with these people.

                    DONALD
          I won't. Anyway, listen, I meant to ask
          you, I need a cool way to kill people.
                    (off Kaufman's look)
          Don't worry! For my script.

                    KAUFMAN
          I don't write that kind of stuff.

                    DONALD
          Oh, come on, man, please? You're the
          genius.

                    KAUFMAN
          Here you go. The killer's a literature
          professor. He cuts off little chunks
          from his victim's bodies until they die.
          He calls himself "The Deconstructionist".

                    DONALD
          That's kinda good. I like that.

                    KAUFMAN
          See, I was kidding, Donald.

                    DONALD
          Oh, okay. Sorry. You got me.
                    (beat)
          Do you mind if I use it, though?

INT. LIVING ROOM - DAY

Donald types at his desk. Caroline lounges in a nearby chair
reading script pages.

                    CAROLINE
          It's really good!

                    DONALD
          You know what I did was, I tried to split
          the Cassie scene in half --

                    CAROLINE
          I know, I saw that. Why did you do that?

                    DONALD
          Because I wanted there to be more
          tension.

INT. EMPTY LIVING ROOM - DAY

Kaufman is staring at a blank sheet of typewriter paper,
listening to Caroline and Donald.

                    DONALD (O.S.)
          You know?

                    CAROLINE (O.S.)
          That's great.

                    DONALD (O.S.)
          And then you pick it up later. It keeps
          more tension. That way the audience gets
          hooked early on.

                    CAROLINE (O.S.)
          Yeah?

                    DONALD (O.S.)
          You like it?

                    CAROLINE (O.S.)
          I *really* like it.

                    DONALD (O.S.)
          Yeah?

INT. PARTY - NIGHT

Another party. Kaufman makes his way through the crowded
room toward Donald in the corner with Caroline.

                    DONALD
          You look hot tonight, baby.

                    CAROLINE
          Thanks, Donald. That's swell of you to
          say.

Kaufman approaches.

                    DONALD
               (to Kaufman)
          Don't you think she's hot, bro?

                    KAUFMAN
          I'm heading home, Donald.

                    DONALD
          Really? Come on.
               (looking off)
          Hey, it's Amelia!

                                        (CONTINUED)

CONTINUED:

Kaufman turns, surprised and panicky.

                    DONALD (CONT'D)
          Amelia!

Amelia looks over. She spots Kaufman and Donald. She's with
a guy.

                    AMELIA
          Hey, Donald!
               (beat)
          Hi, Charlie.

                    KAUFMAN
          Oh, hey, hi there.

                    DONALD
               (hugging her)
          God, Amelia, we don't see you anymore.
          What happened to you?

                    AMELIA
               (laughing)
          It's good to see you.

                    DONALD
          Oh, this is my girlfriend, Caroline.
          She's a makeup artist for the movies.

                    CAROLINE
          Hi.

                    AMELIA
          Hi. Um...this is David, my friend.

                    KAUFMAN
          Hi.

                    DAVID
          Hey. Nice to meet you. Amelia's talked
          a lot about you.

                    DONALD
          Hi, I'm Donald.

                    DAVID
          Hey.

                    CAROLINE
          Caroline.

                    DAVID
          Hi.

(CONTINUED)

CONTINUED: (2)

                    DONALD
          Heeey...cool camera.

Donald, Caroline and David get involved in the camera.

                    AMELIA
               (to Kaufman)
          So, how are you?

                    DAVID
               (to Donald)
          Uh, yeah, thanks...I was just shooting a
          little at the party here, just for fun.

                    KAUFMAN
               (to Amelia)
          Well, you know me, a mess.

                    AMELIA
          Oh, Charlie. It's really good to see
          you.
               (beat)
          Is the work good?

                    KAUFMAN
          It's a disaster. I don't know what I'm
          doing. But, anyway, it's my problem. I
          don't want to bore you. I mean, you have
          your own stuff...right?

Amelia looks hurt.

                    KAUFMAN (CONT'D)
          I mean we both have our own separate
          stuff. Anyway, I should go. I was just
          heading home to do some work.
               (to Donald)
          You coming?

                    DONALD
          No, man. I'm gonna stay at Caroline's
          tonight. A little push-push in the bush!

                    CAROLINE
               (laughing)
          Donald, you're such a 'tard!

Kaufman hurries off. Amelia watches him go.

INT. EMPTY BEDROOM - NIGHT

A depressed Kaufman fishes on his floor through an ever
increasing pile of books: about turtles, mirror resilvering,
fish, etc. He finds <u>The Portable Darwin</u>. The cover features
a daguerreotype of Darwin. Kaufman paces and reads.

                    KAUFMAN (VOICE OVER)
        To write about a flower, to dramatize a
        flower, I have to show the flower's arc.

VARIOUS BOOKS COVERS: <u>All About Orchids</u>, <u>Orchid Basics</u>...

                KAUFMAN (VOICE OVER) (CONT'D)
        And the flower's arc stretches back to
        the beginning of life. How did this
        flower get here? What was its journey?

INT. BOOK-LINED STUDY - NIGHT

<u>TITLE</u>: ENGLAND, ONE HUNDRED AND THIRTY NINE YEARS EARLIER

Sepia. A sickly Darwin writes at his desk.

                   DARWIN (VOICE OVER)
        Therefore, I should infer from analogy
        that probably all the organic beings
        which have ever lived on this earth have
        descended from some one primordial form
        into which life was first breathed.

INT. EMPTY BEDROOM - CONTINUOUS

Kaufman paces.

                    KAUFMAN (VOICE OVER)
        It is a journey of evolution.
        Adaptation. The journey we all take. A
        journey that unites each and every one of
        us.

INT. DARWIN'S STUDY - NIGHT

Darwin writes.

                    KAUFMAN (VOICE OVER)
        Darwin writes that we all come from the
        very first single cell organism...

EXT. PARKING LOT - DAY

Kaufman gets into his car.

                                    (CONTINUED)

CONTINUED:

                    KAUFMAN (VOICE OVER)
          ...Yet here I am...

EXT. NURSERY - DAY

Laroche works on his plants.

                    KAUFMAN (VOICE OVER)
          ...And there's Laroche...

INT. ORLEAN'S STUDY - NIGHT

Orlean types.

                    KAUFMAN (VOICE OVER)
          ...And there's Orlean...

CLOSE-UP OF GHOST ORCHID

                    KAUFMAN (VOICE OVER)
          ...And there's the ghost orchid...

INT. EMPTY BEDROOM - NIGHT

Kaufman looks off into space, thinking. Silence.

                    KAUFMAN (VOICE OVER)
          ...All trapped in our own bodies, in
          moments in history. That's it. That's
          what I need to do. Tie all of history
          together!

He grabs his mini-recorder and paces like a caged animal.

                    KAUFMAN (CONT'D)
               (into tape recorder)
          Start right before life begins on the
          planet. All is...lifeless. And then,
          like, life begins. Um...with organisms.
          Those little single cell ones. Oh, and
          it's before sex, 'cause, like, everything
          was asexual. Uh, from there we go to
          bigger things. Jellyfish. And then that
          fish that got legs on it and crawled out
          on the land. And then we see, you know,
          like, um, dinosaurs. And then they're
          around for a long, long time. And then,
          and then an asteroid comes and, and
               (making explosion sound)
          Phwark!

INT. EMPTY LIVING ROOM - NIGHT

As he listens to the tape recorded playback of his idea, he slowly shifts from unbridled enthusiasm to a bottomless pit of depression.

>   KAUFMAN
>   (on tape player)
>   --the insects, the simple mammals, the
>   primates, monkeys-- The simple monkeys.
>   The, the old-fashioned monkeys giving way
>   to the new monkeys. Whatever. And then
>   apes-- Whatever. And, and man. Then we
>   see the whole history of human
>   civilization -- hunting and gathering,
>   farming, uh, Bronze Age, war, love,
>   religion, heartache, disease, loneliness,
>   technology. And we bring it all the way
>   to this moment in history...

The taped voice continues. Kaufman stares despondently out the window, into the night.

>   KAUFMAN (CONT'D)
>   (on tape player)
>   ...and end with Susan Orlean in her
>   office at The New Yorker, writing about
>   flowers, and bang! The movie begins.
>   This is great! This is the breakthrough
>   I've been hoping for. It ties everything
>   together. It's profound. It's --

The front door bursts open and Donald charges in. Kaufman quickly clicks off the recorder.

>   DONALD
>   (shouting)
>   McKee is a genius! And hilarious. He
>   just comes up with all these great jokes,
>   and everybody laughs. But he's serious,
>   too, Charles. You'd love him. He's all
>   for originality, just like you. But he
>   says we have to realize that we all write
>   in a genre, and we must find our
>   originality within that genre. See, it
>   turns out there hasn't been a new genre
>   since Fellini invented the mockumentary.
>   My genre's thriller. What's yours?

Kaufman sits. Donald waits for a response, heaving with excitement. No response from Kaufman.

(CONTINUED)

CONTINUED:

                          KAUFMAN
                    (muttering)
               You and I share the same D.N.A. Is there
               anything more lonely than that?

                          DONALD
               What'd you say, bro?

INT. LAROCHE'S LIVING ROOM - NIGHT

Laroche and his father watch TV. The phone rings and Laroche
picks up.

                          LAROCHE
               Yeah?

                          ORLEAN (O.S.)
                    (over telephone)
               Hey.

                          LAROCHE
               Hey, Susie-Q. What you up to?

INT. ORLEAN'S APARTMENT - CONTINUOUS

Orlean lies on her bed in her underwear.

                          ORLEAN
                    (into telephone)
               Well, I don't want to bother you. Just
               thought I'd call and get some more info.

INT. LAROCHE'S LIVING ROOM - CONTINUOUS

                          ORLEAN (O.S.)
                    (over telephone)
               I think you say some pretty smart things,
               John.

                          LAROCHE
               Yeah, smartest guy I know, huh?

INT. ORLEAN'S APARTMENT - CONTINUOUS

                          ORLEAN
                    (into telephone)
               So... whatever happened to your nursery?

INT. LAROCHE'S LIVING ROOM - CONTINUOUS

Laroche glances at the TV. On top is a framed photos of
Laroche's mother.

                                             (CONTINUED)

CONTINUED:

                    LAROCHE
                (into telephone)
      Oh, it was going pretty well, but, you
      know, sometimes bad things happen.
      Darkness descends.

INT. LAROCHE'S CAR - A FEW MOMENTS LATER

Laroche, his wife, his mother, and his uncle pile into a nice
new American car, his wife in front, his mother and uncle in
back. Laroche backs into traffic.

TITLE: NORTH MIAMI NINE YEARS EARLIER

                    UNCLE JIM
      Nursery business good, Johnny?

                    LAROCHE (NON V.O.)
      Everything's good, Uncle Jim. This last
      year's been a dream. I'm tellin' ya.
      We're finally pulling out of debt.

                    MOTHER
      Amen, honey. I'm so proud of you two and--

Laroche smiles back at his mother. A screech of tires and
another car crashes head on into theirs. Laroche's face
smacks the steering wheel, his front teeth fly in all
directions. His mother rockets forward smashing through the
windshield. His uncle hits Laroche's wife in the head,
jerking her forward and landing on top of her.

EXT. STREET - DAY

The aftermath of the accident: police, ambulances, the two
wrecked cars, shattered glass, the street blocked-off.
Laroche is strapped to a stretcher on the ground, his face
banged up; his front teeth gone, his neck immobilized. As an
EMT hovers over, attending to him, Laroche desperately tries
to turn his head to look at the mess but can't. Out of the
corner of his eye he can see two bodies on the ground covered
with sheets.

                    LAROCHE
      Which ones are dead?

                    EMT
      Sir, please don't move your head.

                    LAROCHE
                (sobbing)
      Tell me, which ones are dead? Which ones
      are dead?

INT. HOSPITAL ROOM - DAY

Laroche, in his mourning suit, sits by his comatose wife.

>   LAROCHE (VOICE OVER)
>   I killed my mom, you know...and my uncle.
>   Um... that's how I lost my front teeth.
>   (chuckles)
>   And my wife was in a coma for like, three
>   weeks.

EXT. LAROCHE'S HOUSE - NIGHT

It's dark. Laroche, on the cordless phone, stares out at the
street where the accident took place.

>   LAROCHE
>   And she divorced me, you know, soon after
>   she regained consciousness.

INT. ORLEAN'S APARTMENT - CONTINUOUS

Orlean is crying hard now. She has the phone mouthpiece
flipped up so she can't be heard. She regains control and
flips it down to talk.

>   ORLEAN
>   Well, I think if I almost died, I would
>   leave my marriage, too.

>   LAROCHE (O.S.)
>   (over telephone)
>   Why?

>   ORLEAN
>   Because I could. Because it's like a
>   free pass. Nobody can judge you if you
>   almost died.

INT. LAROCHE'S ROOM - CONTINUOUS

Laroche, on the phone, sits at his desk in front of many
photos of orchids tacked to the wall.

>   LAROCHE
>   Well, I judged her. Maybe I was being
>   judged, too.

EXT. STREET - DAY

Laroche walks through a field where the remains of his
greenhouse are scattered about: glass, wood, and the green
pulp that was once plant life.

(CONTINUED)

CONTINUED:

> LAROCHE (VOICE OVER)
> Like a month after that, Hurricane Andrew
> came along and just swooped down like an
> angel of God and wiped out everything I
> had left. Everything.

INT. ORLEAN'S ROOM - NIGHT

Orlean listens.

> LAROCHE (O.S.)
> (over telephone)
> I knew it'd break my heart to start
> another nursery, so...

INT. LAROCHE'S ROOM - NIGHT

Laroche stares off.

> LAROCHE
> (into telephone)
> ...you know, when the Seminoles called,
> and they wanted a white guy, an expert,
> to get their nursery going. I took the
> job. I wasn't gonna give 'em a
> conventional little potted plant place.
> I was gonna give 'em something amazing,
> y'know?

> ORLEAN (O.S.)
> (over telephone)
> Yeah, I know, John. I know.

INT. RESTAURANT - MIDDAY

Busy lunch crowd. Valerie sits at a table with Orlean and an
open New Yorker magazine.

> VALERIE
> (reading)
> "I was going to give them something
> amazing."
> (looking up)
> ...It's beautifully written. You have
> such a unique voice.

> ORLEAN
> Thank you very much.

> VALERIE
> We're big fans.

(CONTINUED)

CONTINUED:

              ORLEAN
Oh, thank you.

              VALERIE
Laroche is such a fun character.

              ORLEAN
Yeah. John is a fun character all right.

              VALERIE
It's funny and fresh. And sad in a way.
So we were wondering, what's next?

              ORLEAN
Well, um...Random House has asked me to
expand it into a book, so I'm going to be
doing that.

              VALERIE
Oh.

              ORLEAN
And--

              VALERIE
Susan, we would really like to option
this.

              ORLEAN
You want to make it into a movie?

              VALERIE
Into a movie.

              ORLEAN
    (laughing)
Oh, God! Oh, that's really....

              VALERIE
How does that sound?

              ORLEAN
    (laughing)
That's very exciting.

              VALERIE
Good.

              ORLEAN
It's just comical. I mean, I hadn't
thought of it. I've never written a
screenplay before, so --

CONTINUED: (2)

> VALERIE
> Oh, don't worry about that. We have
> screenwriters to write the screenplay.
> You needn't worry about that.

INT. EMPTY BEDROOM - DAY

Kaufman sits on the floor amidst messy piles of books and
papers. The answering machine picks up the ringing
telephone.

> MARTY
> (on answering machine)
> Hey, superstar! It's Marty, super-agent.
> I just wanted to remind you it's been
> thirteen weeks, and Valerie's anxious to
> see a draft. So if you could wrap things
> up, get it to her by Monday, that'd be
> great. Call me when you get this.
> Adios, amigo.

INT. VALERIE'S APARTMENT - NIGHT

Valerie, in bed in a white T-shirt and reading glasses,
studies some script pages. The bathroom door opens and
Charlie emerges in pajamas. He sits down next to her, reads
over her shoulder. She doesn't look up.

As she continues to read, with no change of expression, she
drapes one of her legs over his. He studies the line of her
neck. She feels it, gets a little smile on her face,
continues to read. She laughs at something in the script.

> KAUFMAN
> What? What'd you laugh at?

> VALERIE
> You're a genius.

> KAUFMAN
> Which line?

> VALERIE
> You're a genius. You're a genius.

He cranes closer to see. She leans in and kisses him, pulls
herself on top of him, straddles him. He looks up at her
towering over him. She tosses the script on the floor.

INT. EMPTY BEDROOM - DAY

Kaufman, alone in bed, ejaculates. He lies there. After a
few moments, he gets up and sits naked in front of his
typewriter. He reads the page.

                    KAUFMAN (VOICE OVER)
          "We see orchid hunter...Augustus Margary.
          He wears a filthy, spittle-soaked rag
          around his head to quell the excruciating
          pain. The back of his trousers are
          stained greasy black from an anal leakage
          due to dysentery. He moans with each
          tentative step through the sickeningly
          overgrown jungle." I'm fucked.

                                                  CUT TO:

MONTAGE

Jumble of images: Laroche talking, flowers, Indians, Orlean,
the trial. The rapid-fire click-click of typing.

                    KAUFMAN (VOICE OVER)
          Okay, we open with Laroche. He's funny.
          Okay, he says-- Okay, he says "I love to
          mutate plants." He says "Mutation is
          fun." Okay, we show flowers and.... Okay
          we have to have the court case. Okay, we
          show Laroche. Okay, he says, "I was
          mutatated as a baby. That's why I'm so
          smart." That's funny. Okay, we open at
          the beginning of time. No. Okay we open
          with Laroche driving into the swamp.

                    LAROCHE
          Cra-a-azy White Man!

INT. EMPTY BEDROOM - NIGHT

Kaufman awakes with a start. Donald and Caroline are playing
off-screen.

                    DONALD
               (muffled through door)
          Gonna get you. Jelly belly! Jelly belly
          gonna get you!

                    CAROLINE
               (muffled through door)
               (laughing)
          Stop it!

                                              (CONTINUED)

CONTINUED:

Kaufman peers through the darkness at all the books, papers, coffee cups. He picks up <u>The Orchid Thief</u>, opens it, reads.

INT. AGENT'S OFFICE - DAY

Kaufman sits with his agent Marty in a glass-walled office.

> KAUFMAN
> I don't know how to adapt this. I mean, I should just have stuck with my own stuff. I don't know why I thought I could write this.

> MARTY
> See her?

Marty waves at a passing beauty. She waves back, keeps walking. Kaufman follows the girl's ass with his eyes.

> MARTY (CONT'D)
> I fucked her up the ass.
>   (pause)
> No. I'm kidding.
>   (awkwardly)
> Um...maybe I can help.

Kaufman looks at Marty. Will he accept help from an agent?

> KAUFMAN
> It's about flowers.

> MARTY
> Okay. Um...but it, it's not only about flowers, right? I mean, you have the crazy plant nut guy, right? He's funny. Right?

Kaufman pulls out a folded newspaper clipping, reads:

> KAUFMAN
>   (reading)
> "There's not...nearly enough of him to fill a book, so Orlean...digresses in long passages." Blah, blah, blah. "No narrative really unites these passages." New York Times Book Review. I can't structure this. It's that sprawling New Yorker shit.

Marty gets distracted by another sexy woman walking by.

CONTINUED:

> MARTY
> Oh, man. I'd fuck her up the ass.
> (looking back)
> Sorry.

> KAUFMAN
> The book has no story. There's no story!

> MARTY
> All right. Make one up. I mean, nobody
> in this town can make up a crazy story
> like you. You're the king of that.

> KAUFMAN
> No, I didn't want to do that this time.
> It's someone else's material. I have a
> responsibility to Susan -- Anyway, I
> wanted to grow as a writer. I wanted to
> do something simple. Show people how
> amazing flowers are.

> MARTY
> Are they amazing?

> KAUFMAN
> I don't know. I think they are.

MARTY chuckles

> KAUFMAN (CONT'D)
> I need you to get me out of this.

> MARTY
> Charlie you've been stringing them along
> for months now. Not to give them
> anything at this point would be a
> terrible career move.

INT. EMPTY HOUSE - NIGHT

Kaufman enters and heads to the stairs. Donald, typing
furiously at his desk, looks up.

> DONALD
> (calling to Kaufman)
> Hey, my script's going amazing! Right
> now I'm working out an Image System.
> Because of my multiple personality theme,
> I've chosen the motif of broken mirrors
> to show my protagonists's fragmented
> self. Bob says an Image System greatly
> increases the complexity of an aesthetic
> emotion. Bob says --

(CONTINUED)

CONTINUED:

                     KAUFMAN
You sound like you're in a cult.

                     DONALD
No, it's just good writing technique.
Oh, I made you a copy of McKee's Ten
Commandments!

Kaufman disappears upstairs.

INT. EMPTY BEDROOM - CONTINUOUS

Kaufman enters, sees the McKee Ten Commandments taped to his
wall.

                     DONALD
I posted one over both our work areas!

Kaufman tears down the Ten Commandments. Donald appears
backlit in the doorway and seems oddly threatening.

                  DONALD (CONT'D)
You shouldn't have done that.

They look at each other. Donald breaks the tension, smiles.

                  DONALD (CONT'D)
                 (laughing)
'Cause it's extremely helpful. Hey,
Charles, I'm putting a song in. "Happy
Together." Like when characters sing pop
songs in their pajamas and dance around.
I thought it'd be a nice way to break the
tension. At first I was nervous about
putting a song in a thriller, but Bob
says that "Casablanca", one of the
greatest screenplays ever written, did
exactly that. Mixed genres.

                     KAUFMAN
I haven't slept in a week, Donald. I
need to go to bed.

                     DONALD
Oh. Okay. Good night.

Donald remains on the floor.

INT. HOTEL ROOM - NIGHT

Orlean is on the phone. She is shaky and drunk.

                                     (CONTINUED)

CONTINUED:

                    LAROCHE (O.S.)
                (over telephone)
          Yeah?

                    ORLEAN
          Hi. John, it's Susan again.

                    LAROCHE (O.S.)
          Hey, Susie-Q!

                    ORLEAN
          Um...how's it going?

INT. LITTLE BOY'S BEDROOM - CONTINUOUS

The room is now filled with computer equipment. Posters of
naked women adorn the walls.

                    LAROCHE
                (into telephone)
          Great! I'm training myself on the
          Internet. It's fascinating. I'm doing
          pornography. It's amazing how much these
          suckers'll pay for photographs of chicks.
          It doesn't matter if they're fat or ugly
          or what.

                    ORLEAN (O.S.)
                (over telephone)
          Well, that sounds good.

                    LAROCHE
          No, it's great is what it is.

                    ORLEAN (O.S.)
                (over telephone)
          Listen, John...

INT. ORLEAN'S HOTEL ROOM - CONTINUOUS

                    ORLEAN
                (into telephone)
          ...I hate feeling like I'm being a pain
          to you, but I...I still haven't seen a
          ghost.

INT. LAROCHE'S ROOM - CONTINUOUS

                    LAROCHE
                (into telephone)
          Yeah?

                                        (CONTINUED)

CONTINUED:

                         ORLEAN (O.S.)
                    (over telephone)
               And I was hoping maybe
               you'd...

                         LAROCHE
               Yeah. Yeah, I'll take you in.

INT. ORLEAN'S HOTEL ROOM - CONTINUOUS

                         LAROCHE (O.S.)
                    (over telephone)
               Tomorrow.

                         ORLEAN
                    (into telephone)
               Really? Oh, thank you so much! Oh,
               John!

INT. EMPTY BEDROOM - LATER

Kaufman lies half-awake in bed, sweating, his eyes darting
back and forth. He looks over at the clock. It's 3:32.

                         KAUFMAN
               Damn it.

Kaufman switches on a lamp, pulls The Orchid Thief from his
bag, flips through it. There are now many yellow hi-lited
passages. He reads one.

                         ORLEAN (VOICE OVER)
               There are too many ideas and things and
               people. Too many directions to go. I
               was starting to believe the reason it
               matters to care passionately about
               something is that it whittles the world
               down to a more manageable size.

                         KAUFMAN
               Such sweet, sad insights. So true.

Kaufman flips to the glowing, smiling author photo.

                         KAUFMAN (CONT'D)
               I like looking at you.

He stares at the photo. Its smile broadens. It talks.

                         ORLEAN
               I like looking at you, too, Charlie.

CONTINUED:

The photo smiles warmly at him. Kaufman closes his eyes, begins to jerk-off.

Then: Kaufman and Orlean are in his bed together, making love. She smiles at him throughout. They finish.

Then: Kaufman is alone in bed, heaving. He looks at the still smiling photo. It seems somehow sleepy now.

>   KAUFMAN
>   I don't know how to do this. I'm afraid
>   I'll disappoint you. You've written a
>   beautiful book. I can't sleep. I'm
>   losing my hair. I'm fat and repulsive.

>   ORLEAN
>   Shhhh! You're not. You're not. Just
>   whittle it down. Focus on one thing in
>   the story. Just find the one thing that
>   you care passionately about ... then
>   write about that.

Kaufman studies her delicate, melancholy face. He's in love.

INT. KITCHEN - MORNING

Kaufman paces and talks animatedly into his mini-recorder.

>   KAUFMAN
>   We see Susan Orlean, delicate, haunted by
>   loneliness, fragile, beautiful. She lies
>   awake next to her sleeping, insensitive
>   husband. Her voice-over begins: "I
>   suppose I do have one unembarrassed
>   passion. I want to know how it feels to
>   care about something passionately."

Donald, in his underwear, enters with Caroline. She's in a T-shirt we've seen Donald wearing.

>   DONALD
>   Morning.

Kaufman looks up, sees Caroline with Donald, smiles.

>   KAUFMAN
>   Hey, you two. Up early for a change.

>   DONALD
>   You seem chipper.

>   KAUFMAN
>   I'm good. I have some new ideas.

CONTINUED:

                    CAROLINE
          Oh, God, you guys are so smart! It's
          like a brain factory in here.

                    DONALD
          I got some ideas, too, this morning.

                    CAROLINE
          He got really, really good ones. You
          know, in a Donald sort of way.

Caroline giggles.

                    DONALD
          I'm putting in a chase sequence. So the
          killer flees on horseback with the girl.
          Cop's after them on a motorcycle. And
          it's like a battle between motors and
          horses. Like technology versus horse.

                    KAUFMAN
          And they're still all one person, right?

                    CAROLINE
          Well, that's the big pay-off.

                    KAUFMAN
               (sincerely)
          It sounds exciting.

                    DONALD
          Thanks, man. Thanks.

                    CAROLINE
               (to Donald)
          See, I told you he was gonna like it.

Caroline gives him a loud kiss. Kaufman watches them.

                    DONALD
          You're my muse.

                    CAROLINE
               (kissing him and giggling)
          Mm-hm.

                    DONALD
          You are.

                    CAROLINE
          I love being your muse.

INT. L.A. BUSINESS LUNCH RESTAURANT - DAY

Kaufman enters and approaches the hostess.

                    KAUFMAN
          I'm picking up an order for Kaufman.

He hands the hostess his credit card and she smiles and walks
off to get his order. An uncharacteristically happy Kaufman
scans the busy restaurant. He spots Valerie alone at a
table. Oh shit. He wants to move out of view. He spots
some chairs near the door and heads for them, glancing over
at Valerie as he does. She's looking at him. She smiles and
waves. He does the same and heads over to the table.

                    KAUFMAN (CONT'D)
          Oh...Hi.

                    VALERIE
          Hi, Charlie. Hey, it's quite a
          coincidence bumping into you.

                    KAUFMAN
          I'm sorry I didn't call you back. I was
          away last week. I planned to.

                    VALERIE
          That's okay --

                    KAUFMAN
          I meant to, because, things are going
          really well now and I wanted to let you
          know.

                    VALERIE
          Oh, well, that's great. I mean, I'm
          really anxious to see something.

                    KAUFMAN
          Okay. Good.

                    VALERIE
          But listen, you should sit down because
          I'm here with Susan right now. And she's
          dying to meet you, so it's funny bumping
          into you.

                    KAUFMAN
          Susan Orlean is here?

                    VALERIE
          Yes, she's in town for a reading or
          something.

(CONTINUED)

CONTINUED:

                    KAUFMAN
          Oh.

                    VALERIE
          Anyway, she's just on the phone. Have a
          seat. She's dying to meet you.

Kaufman looks off to the restroom area.

                    KAUFMAN
          Oh, um, well, I should probably go,
          because, well, I'd love to meet her, too,
          but I don't want to be...beholden.
          And... Because once you meet somebody
          that you're writing about it becomes very
          hard to...separate.

                    VALERIE
          Uh-huh.

                    KAUFMAN
          So, well, okay, but I'll speak to you
          soon. And I'm almost done.

                    VALERIE
          Okay.

                    KAUFMAN
          And please tell Susan that I would love
          to meet with her at a future date. As
          she sees fit.

Kaufman exits without his food or credit card.

INT. KAUFMAN'S CAR - DAY

Parked in a strip mall parking lot. Kaufman stuffs his mouth
with fast food. He is agitated and humiliated.

                    KAUFMAN (VOICE OVER)
          Who am I kidding? This is not Susan
          Orlean's story. I have no connection
          with her. I can't even meet her. I can't
          meet anyone. I have no understanding of
          anything outside of my own panic and self-
          loathing and pathetic, little existence.
          It's like the only thing I'm actually
          qualified to write about is myself and my
          own self --

His eyes light up.

INT. EMPTY BEDROOM - DAY

Kaufman paces with great energy and speaks into a handheld
tape recorder.

                    KAUFMAN
              (into tape recorder)
         We open on Charlie Kaufman, fat, old,
         bald, repulsive, sitting in a Hollywood
         restaurant across from Valerie Thomas, a
         lovely, statuesque film executive.
         Kaufman, trying to get a writing
         assignment... wanting to impress her,
         sweats profusely.

Later: Kaufman lies on his bed, trying to wrap his head
around this new direction.

                    KAUFMAN (CONT'D)
              (into tape recorder)
         Fat, bald Kaufman paces furiously in his
         bedroom. He speaks into his hand-held
         tape recorder, and says "Charlie Kaufman,
         fat, bald, repulsive, old, sits at a
         Hollywood restaurant with Valerie
         Thomas..."

Later: Kaufman types as a cassette recorder plays.

                    KAUFMAN (CONT'D)
              (voice on tape recorder)
         Kaufman, repugnant, ridiculous, jerks off
         to the book jacket photo of Susan Or--

Donald appears in the doorway with a script.

                    KAUFMAN (CONT'D)
         What? What do you want?

                    DONALD
         I've finished my script. I'm done. So
         would you show it to your agent? It's
         called "The Three."

Kaufman grabs Donald's script and throws it on his bed. The
Three is printed on the cover in some dramatic bold typeface.

                    DONALD (CONT'D)
         Thanks. I also want to thank you for
         your idea. It was very helpful. I
         changed it a little. Now the killer cuts
         off body pieces and makes his victims eat
         them. It's kind of like...
                    (MORE)

                                              (CONTINUED)

CONTINUED:

                    DONALD (CONT'D)
          Caroline has this great tattoo of a snake
          swallowing its own tail and --

Kaufman puts his head in his hands

                    KAUFMAN
          Ourobouros.

                    DONALD
          I don't know what that means.

                    KAUFMAN
          The snake. It's called Ourobouros.

                    DONALD
          I don't think so. But, anyway, it's cool
          for my killer to have this modus
          operandi. Because at the end when he
          forces the woman who's really him to eat
          herself, he's also eating himself to
          death.

                    KAUFMAN
          I'm insane. I'm Ourobouros.

                    DONALD
          I don't know what that word means.

                    KAUFMAN
          I've written myself into my screenplay.

                    DONALD
          Oh. That's kinda weird, huh?

                    KAUFMAN
          It's self-indulgent. It's narcissistic.
          It's solipsistic. It's pathetic. I'm
          pathetic. I'm fat and pathetic.

                    DONALD
          I'm sure you had good reasons, Charles.
          You're an artist.

                    KAUFMAN
          The reason is because I'm too timid to
          speak to the woman who wrote the book.
          Because I'm pathetic. Because I have no
          idea how to write. Because I can't make
          flowers fascinating. Because I suck.

                    DONALD
          Hey, am I in the script?

                                        (CONTINUED)

CONTINUED: (2)

                    KAUFMAN
          I'm going to New York. I'll meet her.
          That's it. That's what I have to do.

                    DONALD
          Don't get mad at me for saying this,
          Charles, but Bob's having a seminar in
          New York this weekend. So if you're
          stuck....

Kaufman shoots Donald a look, exits without a word.

INT. VAN - DAY

Laroche drives. Orlean holds on, but seems to be enjoying
herself now.

                    ORLEAN
          ... and she said, "Oh, Laroche is such a
          fun character."

                    LAROCHE
          No shit, I'm a fun character.

Orlean laughs.

                    LAROCHE (CONT'D)
          Who's gonna play me?

                    ORLEAN
          Oh, well, I've gotta write the book
          first, John. Then, you know, they get
          somebody to write the screenplay.

                    LAROCHE
          Hey, I think I should play me.

Orlean laughs, charmed.

EXT. SWAMP - DAY

Laroche leads Orlean through the waist-high swamp water.

                    ORLEAN (VOICE OVER)
          Most people yearn for something
          exceptional something so inspiring that
          they'd want to risk everything for that
          passion. But few would act on it. It
          was very powerful. And it's intoxicating
          to be around someone so alive.

(CONTINUED)

CONTINUED:

                      LAROCHE
                (calling back)
        Come on, just follow me! They're right
        nearby.

                      ORLEAN
        Okay.

Later: They've been walking for a long while. It's hot and
miserable. They don't seem to be finding anything.

                      ORLEAN (CONT'D)
        Can I ask you a personal question?

                      LAROCHE
        Look, we're not lost!

They walk on.

                      LAROCHE (CONT'D)
        I've done this a million times. When
        everything is killing me, I just say
        "screw it," and go straight ahead.

EXT. SWAMP - LATER

The sun is high. Orlean and Laroche sit on dry ground. She
stares at him. He won't look at her, but busies himself
opening the backpack and pulling out food. He picks up a
small stick.

                      LAROCHE
                (jamming stick into the ground)
        Sundial! I'll just set this up, we'll
        wait a few minutes. Then we'll be able
        to tell which way the sun's moving. We
        should be headed southeast...

She stares down at him. He busies himself adjusting the
stick to avoid eye contact.

                      LAROCHE (CONT'D)
        So...you collect anything?

He turns to her, knocks over the stick, fixes it.

                      ORLEAN
        Not really, no.

                      LAROCHE
        Yeah, well, you know it's not really
        about collecting the thing. It's about
        being able to...
                (MORE)

(CONTINUED)

CONTINUED:

                    LAROCHE (CONT'D)
          You know the thing about computers, the
          thing I like, is that I'm immersed in
          'em, but...it's not like a living thing
          that's gonna leave or die or something.

Orlean stares at the twig in the ground. She looks at
Laroche. Laroche looks down and fiddles with the twig.
Laroche smiles sheepishly at Orlean. Rage and panic sweep
across her face, her fists clench into balls. Her eyes
become wild, some dark fantasy plays out in her brain.
Laroche seems unaware. Silence.

                    ORLEAN
          John, I'm sorry. I just --

Laroche gets up angrily and sloshes off through the water.

                    LAROCHE
          Hey. Okay. Fuck the sundial. I know
          how to get outta here. I know how to get
          outta here. I know this swamp like the
          back of my goddamn hand! You're just
          like everybody else. Fucking leeches!
          You just attach yourself to me and...suck
          me dry, spit me out. You know, why don't
          you get your own fucking life? Your own
          fucking interests? Fucking spoiled
          bitch!

EXT. SWAMP - DAY

Laroche and Orlean slog through the water with purpose,
looking only straight ahead. As they walk the sounds and
colors become subdued. Soon there is silence.

                    ORLEAN (VOICE OVER)
          Life seemed to be filled with things that
          were just like the ghost orchid.
          Wonderful to imagine and...easy to fall
          in love with, but a little fantastic
          ...and fleeting...and out of reach.

They turn left and see metal flashing in the sunlight.
Orlean and Laroche walk toward the car.

INT. AIRPLANE - NIGHT

A morose Kaufman reads The Orchid Thief.

TITLE: THREE YEARS LATER

                    KAUFMAN (VOICE OVER)
          (reading) "...but a little fantastic and
          fleeting...and out of reach."

                                        (CONTINUED)

CONTINUED:

Kaufman is deeply moved. He hi-lites the passage, then looks
at the smiling photo of Orlean. He finds himself lost in it.

EXT. NYC STREET - DAY

Kaufman arrives at the New Yorker building and enters with
steely determination.

INT. ELEVATOR - DAY

Kaufman rides up in the crowded elevator. It stops a few
times; people get off and on. Kaufman sweats. The doors
open again. The New Yorker logo is painted on the wall
opposite the elevator. Nobody gets off or on. The doors
close. The elevator continues up. Kaufman hates himself.
Soon the elevator is emptied out with the exception of
Kaufman. It begins its descent and stops once again at the
New Yorker. This time Orlean gets on. Kaufman is panicked.
Orlean looks at him blankly, presses "lobby", and faces
front. Kaufman sweats, studies the back of her head. The
elevator arrives at the lobby. Orlean gets out. Kaufman
hesitates.

INT. HOTEL ROOM - NIGHT

Kaufman types from his notes, reads what he has written.
He's frustrated, hysterical. He paces, yanks the sheets from
the bed, tries to tear them, swings them wildly, knocking
over a bedside lamp and shattering the bulb. He stops,
heaves, bends to pick up the broken glass. The phone rings.
He answers it, still holding the glass.

                    KAUFMAN
          Um, hello?

INT. MARTY'S OFFICE - DAY

Marty on the phone.

                    MARTY
               (into telephone)
          Hey, it's Marty. How's it going? Uh,
          has it been helpful talking to the
          writer? What's her name?

                    KAUFMAN (O.S.)
               (over telephone)
          Susan Orlean. It's been okay.

                    MARTY
          Uh-huh. Well, I mean, are, are you, are
          you making headway? Valerie's been
          breathing down my neck.

                                        (CONTINUED)

CONTINUED:

                          KAUFMAN (O.S.)
        You can't rush inspiration.

                          MARTY
        Okay. All right. Fair enough. Listen,
        the other reason I called was "The
        Three"...it's just amazing!

                                          CUT TO:

INT. KAUFMAN'S HOTEL ROOM - CONTINUOUS

                          KAUFMAN
          (into telephone)
        I don't know what that is.

                          MARTY (O.S.)
          (over telephone)
        Donald's script! A smart, edgy thriller.
        It's the best script I've read all year!

                          KAUFMAN
        Oh. Good.

                          MARTY (O.S.)
        Yeah, I'm gonna sell it for a shitload.
        Two fuckin' talented guys in one family!
        In fact, you know, maybe you could bring
        your brother on to help you with the
        orchid thing.

                          KAUFMAN
        Marty, don't say that. I mean --

                          MARTY (O.S.)
        All right. All right. It's just a
        thought, buddy. I mean, he's really
        goddamned amazing at structure.

                          KAUFMAN
        I have to go.

                          MARTY (O.S.)
        All right. Adios, amigo. Finish, finish
        --

Kaufman hangs up phone.

                          KAUFMAN
          (yelling)
        Fuck!!!

INT. AUDITORIUM - A BIT LATER

Kaufman sits in the packed room. McKee enters the stage with
a microphone clipped to his lapel. The audience erupts into
applause.

                    MCKEE
        Okay, thank you, thank you. We have a
        long three days ahead. Years from now
        you'll be standing around a posh cocktail
        party congratulating yourself on how you
        spent an entire weekend locked in a room
        with an asshole from Hollywood for your
        art.

The audience laughs, except for Kaufman who looks pained.

                KAUFMAN (VOICE OVER)
        I am pathetic. I am a loser.

                MCKEE
        So, what is the substance of writing?

MONTAGE - VARIOUS

McKee continues to talk but his voice goes under.

                KAUFMAN (VOICE OVER)
        I have failed. I am panicked. I have
        sold out.

                MCKEE
        Nothing as trivial as words...

                KAUFMAN (VOICE OVER)
        I am worthless. I....

                MCKEE
         (fading out)
        ...is at the heart of this great art...
        first, last...

                KAUFMAN (VOICE OVER)
        Eh, what the fuck am I doing here?

                MCKEE
        ...always, the imperative is to tell a
        story.

                KAUFMAN (VOICE OVER)
        What the fuck am I doing here?! Fuck!
        It is my weakness...

                                    (CONTINUED)

CONTINUED:

                         MCKEE
          Your goal must be a good story well told.

Kaufman watches with disdain as people take notes.

                         KAUFMAN (VOICE OVER)
          ...my ultimate lack of conviction that
          brings me here...

                         MCKEE
          The protagonist needs to pursue the
          object of his conscious or his...

                         KAUFMAN (VOICE OVER)
          ...Easy answers...

                         MCKEE
          ...unconscious desire to the end of the
          line, within the limits established...

                         KAUFMAN (VOICE OVER)
          ...Rules to short-cut yourself to
          success. And here I am, because my
          jaunt...

                         MCKEE
          ...by setting and character.

                         KAUFMAN (VOICE OVER)
          ...into the abyss brought me nothing.
          Well, isn't that just the risk one takes
          for attempting something new?

                         MCKEE
          The measure of the value of the
          character's desire should be in direct
          proportion to the risks he's willing to
          take.

                         KAUFMAN (VOICE OVER)
          I should leave here right now. I'll
          start over. I need to face this project
          head on and --

                         MCKEE
          ... and God help you if you use voice
          over in your work, my friends!

Kaufman looks up, startled. McKee seems to be staring
directly at him.

(CONTINUED)

CONTINUED: (2)

                    MCKEE (CONT'D)

     God help you! It's flaccid, sloppy
     writing! Any idiot can write voice over
     narration to explain the thoughts of the
     character. Okay, that's it. One hour
     for lunch.

EXT. NYC STREET - A FEW MINUTES LATER

Students exit onto the street in groups. Kaufman wanders by
himself. His face is troubled. There is no sound. Then:

                    MCKEE (VOICE OVER)
     ...You cannot have a protagonist without
     desire! It doesn't make any sense! Any
     fucking sense!...

INT. AUDITORIUM - MORNING

McKee talks directly to an unseen student in the audience.

                    MCKEE
     ...You follow? Good.
          (takes a deep breath)
     Anyone else?

Kaufman timidly raises his hand.

                    MCKEE (CONT'D)
          (to Kaufman)
     Yes?

                    KAUFMAN
     Sir, what if a writer is attempting to
     create a story where nothing much
     happens? Where people don't change, they
     don't have any epiphanies. They struggle
     and are frustrated, and nothing is
     resolved. More a reflection of the real
     world.

                    MCKEE
     The real world?

                    KAUFMAN
     Yes, sir.

                    MCKEE
     The real fucking world. First of all,
     you write a screenplay without conflict
     or crisis, you'll bore your audience to
     tears.
          (MORE)

                                          (CONTINUED)

CONTINUED:

                  MCKEE (CONT'D)
Secondly nothing happens in the world?...
Are you out of your fucking mind? People
are murdered every day. There's
genocide, war, corruption. Every fucking
day somewhere in the world, somebody
sacrifices his life to save somebody
else. Every fucking day someone
somewhere makes a conscious decision to
destroy someone else! People find love!
People lose it! For Christ's sake, a
child watches a mother beaten to death on
the steps of a church! Someone goes
hungry! Somebody else betrays his best
friend for a woman! If you can't find
that stuff in life, then you, my friend,
don't know crap about life! And why the
fuck are you wasting my two precious
hours with your movie? I don't have any
use for it! I don't have any bloody use
for it!

                  KAUFMAN
Okay, thanks.

EXT. NYC STREET - NIGHT

The last of the students are filing out. Kaufman waits,
leaning against the building. McKee emerges, carrying his
brown leather bag. A shaky, tired Kaufman approaches him.

                  KAUFMAN
Mr. McKee.

                  MCKEE
Yes?

                  KAUFMAN
I'm the guy you yelled at this morning.

                  MCKEE
I need more.

                  KAUFMAN
I'm the one who thought things didn't
happen in life.

                  MCKEE
Ah. Right. Okay. Nice to see you.

                  KAUFMAN
I need to talk! Mr. McKee, my even
standing here is very scary. I don't
meet people well. But what you said this
morning shook me to the bone.
          (MORE)

                          (CONTINUED)

CONTINUED:

                    KAUFMAN (CONT'D)
          What you said was bigger than my
          screenwriting choices. It was about my
          choices as a human being. Please.

McKee hesitates for a moment, then reaches out and puts his
arm around Kaufman.

                    MCKEE
          Well, y'know, I could sure use a drink,
          my friend.

INT. BAR - NIGHT

Kaufman and McKee sit at a table with beers. Kaufman reads
from his copy of <u>The Orchid Thief</u>.

                    KAUFMAN
               (reading)
          "...but a little fantastic and fleeting
          and out of reach."

Kaufman closes the book. There's a pause.

                    MCKEE
          Then what happens?

                    KAUFMAN
          That's the end of the book. I wanted to
          present it simply, without big character
          arcs or sensationalizing the story. I
          wanted to show flowers as God's miracles.
          I wanted to show that Orlean never saw
          the blooming ghost orchid. It was about
          disappointment.

                    MCKEE
          I see. That's not a movie. You gotta go
          back, put in the drama.

                    KAUFMAN
          I can't go back. I've got pages of false
          starts and wrong approaches. I'm way
          past my deadline.

                    MCKEE
          I'll tell you a secret. The last act
          makes the film. Wow them in the end and
          you got a hit. You can have flaws,
          problems, but wow them in the end and
          you've got a hit. Find an ending. But
          don't cheat. And don't you dare bring in
          a *deus ex machina*. Your characters must
          change. And the change must come from
          them. Do that and you'll be fine.

                                        (CONTINUED)

CONTINUED:

                        KAUFMAN
            You promise?

McKee nods.

                      KAUFMAN'S BEDROOM
                 (hugging McKee)
            Oh, Mr. McKee.

McKee recognizes Kaufman's bulk as he hugs him.

                      MCKEE
            Have you taken my course before?

                      KAUFMAN
            My brother did. My twin brother Donald.
            He's the one who got me to come.

                      MCKEE
            Twin screenwriters?

                      KAUFMAN
            Yeah.

                      MCKEE
            Well, Julius and Philip Epstein, who
            wrote "Casablanca"...

                      KAUFMAN
            Ah.

                      MCKEE
            ...they were twins.

                      KAUFMAN
            You mentioned that in class.

                      MCKEE
            Finest screenplay ever written.

INT. HOTEL ROOM - NIGHT

Kaufman is working. There are papers and books on the floor.
He tries to make sense out of McKee charts and diagrams. He
is frustrated and exhausted. He sighs, thinks, dials the
phone.

                      DONALD (O.S.)
               (over telephone)
            Great writers' residence.

                                    (CONTINUED)

CONTINUED:

                    KAUFMAN
                (into telephone)
    Donald.

                    DONALD (O.S.)
    Hey, how's your trip going? You getting
    it on with that lady journalist, you dog
    you?

                    KAUFMAN
    Yeah. Listen, I'm just calling to say
    congratulations on your script.

                    DONALD (O.S.)
    Isn't that cool? Marty says he can get
    me, like, high-sixes against a mill-five.

                    KAUFMAN
    That's great, Donald.

INT./EXT.- KAUFMAN HOUSE - CONTINUOUS

Donald sits on the floor with Caroline and Catherine Keener.
They drink wine and are in the middle of a board game.

                    DONALD
                (into telephone)
    I want to thank you for all your help.

                    KAUFMAN (O.S.)
                (over telephone)
    I wasn't any help.

                    DONALD
    Oh, come on, you let me stay in your
    place. And, and your integrity inspired
    me to even try. It's been a wild ride.
    Catherine says she really wants to play
    Cassie.

                    CATHERINE KEENER
                (to Donald)
    Oh, pleeease!...

Keener, Caroline, and Donald laugh. Kaufman is silent for a
long moment, taking this all in.

                    CATHERINE KEENER (CONT'D)
    ...Please, Donald?

INT. HOTEL ROOM - CONTINUOUS

Kaufman is pale.

(CONTINUED)

CONTINUED:

                    KAUFMAN
                 (on telephone)
      Catherine Keener? Catherine Keener's in
      my house?

                 DONALD (O.S.)
                 (over telephone)
      Yeah, we're playing Boggle. She's so
      great. You should really hang out with
      her, Charles.

                 KAUFMAN
      Yeah. Um, look, I've been thinking.
      Maybe you'd be interested in hanging out
      with *me* for a few days in New York.

                 DONALD (O.S.)
      Oh, my God, yes!

                 KAUFMAN
      Yeah? I was gonna show my script to some
      people, and...maybe you could read it,
      too, y'know, if you like.

                 DONALD (O.S.)
      Of, of course. I'd be flattered.

                 KAUFMAN
      Okay.

                 DONALD (O.S.)
      Thanks, Charles.

                 KAUFMAN
                 (quickly, before he changes his
                  mind)
      Okay, bye.

INT. HOTEL ROOM - AFTERNOON

Donald lies on his back on the floor intently reading the
script. Kaufman paces. Donald finishes, is quiet.

                 KAUFMAN
      So, like, what would you do?

                 DONALD
      The script kinda makes fun of me, huh?

                 KAUFMAN
      I'm sorry. I was just trying something.

                                      (CONTINUED)

CONTINUED:

                DONALD
Hey, I don't mind. It's funny.

                KAUFMAN
Oh. Good. Okay. So what would you do?

                DONALD
You and me are so different, Charles.
We're different talents.

                KAUFMAN
I know. Just for fun, how would the
great Donald end this script?

                DONALD
    (chuckles)
Shut up. The great Donald.
    (then serious)
I feel like you're missing something.

                KAUFMAN
    (beat)
All right. Like what?

                DONALD
Look. I did a little research on the
airplane.

Donald pulls a copy of The orchid Thief from his bag. He
opens it and reads.

                DONALD (CONT'D)

"Sometimes this kind of story turns out
to be something more...some glimpse of
life that expands like those Japanese
paper balls you drop in water and they
bloom into flowers, and the flower is so
marvelous you can't believe there was a
time all you saw in front of you was a
paper ball and a glass of water." Well,
first of all, that's inconsistent. She,
she said that she didn't care about
flowers.

                KAUFMAN
For God's sake, it's just a metaphor.

                DONALD
But for what? What turned that paper
ball into a flower? It's not in the
book, Charles.

                              (CONTINUED)

CONTINUED: (2)

                        KAUFMAN
            I don't know. You're reaching.

                        DONALD
            Maybe. But I think you actually need to
            speak to this woman. To know her.

                        KAUFMAN
                 (beat)
            I can't. Really.

                        DONALD
            I'll go. I'll pretend I'm you.

Kaufman rolls his eyes.

                        DONALD (CONT'D)
            I want to do it, Charles. We'll get to
            the bottom of this. We're gonna fix your
            movie, bro.

A long silence while Kaufman looks his brother up and down.

                        KAUFMAN
            But you've gotta be exactly me. I have a
            reputation to maintain. You can't be a
            goofball. You can't be an asshole.

                        DONALD
            I'm not an asshole.

                        KAUFMAN
            You know what I mean. No flirting. No
            bad jokes. Don't laugh how you laugh.

                        DONALD
            I'm not gonna laugh. I get to have
            people think I'm you. It's an honor.

INT. ORLEAN'S OFFICE - DAY

Orlean is behind her desk. Donald, dressed as Charlie, sits
across from her, doing his best serious writer impression.
He laughs at something she has said. Then:

                        DONALD
            So, I guess I'll bring out the big guns
            now. Do you keep in touch with Laroche?

                        ORLEAN
            Um....

                                              (CONTINUED)

CONTINUED:

                        DONALD
               The reason I ask is that I felt I
               detected an attraction to him in the
               subtext. Care to comment?

Orlean responds with what might be a practiced casualness.

                        ORLEAN
               Well, our relationship was strictly
               reporter-subject. I mean, certainly an
               intimacy does evolve in this kind of
               relationship.

                        DONALD
               Mm.

                        ORLEAN
               By definition, I was so interested in
               everything he had to say. But the
               relationship ends when the book ends.

Donald scribbles on pad.

                        DONALD
                 (under his breath)
               Mendacious deceit.

                        ORLEAN
               What?

                        DONALD
               Nothing. Uh, I just have one more
               question. If you could have dinner with
               one historical personage, living or dead,
               who would it be?

Orlean is somewhat relieved she's dealing with an idiot.

                        ORLEAN
               Well, I would have to say Einstein. Or
               Jesus.

                        DONALD
               Very good. Interesting answer.

INT. HOTEL ROOM - DAY

Kaufman paces, stares out the window, watches TV. Donald
enters, dressed as Charlie.

                        DONALD
               She's lying!

CONTINUED:

>   KAUFMAN
>   What do you mean? What happened?
>
>   DONALD
>   Nothing. She said everything right. Too
>   right.
>
>   KAUFMAN
>   Well, maybe they're too right because
>   they're true. Did you embarrass me?
>
>   DONALD
>   People who answer questions too right are
>   liars. And everybody says Jesus and
>   Einstein. That's a prepackaged answer.
>
>   KAUFMAN
>   What do you mean, Jesus and Einstein?
>
>   DONALD
>   Listen, Charles, I have an idea. You'll
>   need to buy me a pair of binoculars.
>
>   KAUFMAN
>   What's Jesus and Einstein?

Donald winks, picks up a pen, holds it like a microphone, and
sings and dances around Kaufman, who just stares at him.

>   DONALD
>   (singing)
>   `Imagine me and you, I do. I think about
>   you day and night, it's only right...'
>   (speaking)
>   Come on, sing with me!
>   (singing)
>   `To think about the one you love and hold
>   her tight/So happy together!'
>
>   KAUFMAN
>   What the hell do you need binoculars for?

INT. OFFICE BUILDING HALLWAY - NIGHT

Kaufman nervously watches the elevator doors. Donald stares
through binoculars out the window at the end of the hall.

>   KAUFMAN
>   Let's go, let's go.
>
>   DONALD
>   She hung up the phone. She's upset.

CONTINUED:

                    KAUFMAN
          Stop watching her. Leave her alone.

                    DONALD
          She's crying. She's at her computer.

                    KAUFMAN
          This is morally reprehensible.

                    DONALD
              (reading her computer screen)
          United...to Miami...eleven...fifty-five
          A.M. tomorrow...I thought she was done
          with Laroche.

                    KAUFMAN
          Her parents live in Florida, Donald.

                    DONALD
          That was no parent phone call, my friend.

                    KAUFMAN
          Don't say "my friend."

                    DONALD
          A guy entering. Handsome.

                    KAUFMAN
          Must be her husband.

                    DONALD
          She's acting weird with him, though,
          right? Don't you think? What's she
          hiding from him?
              (thought)
          Maybe she's a lesbian and doesn't know
          how to tell him. What do you think?

INT. HOTEL ROOM - NIGHT

Kaufman reads Story by McKee. Donald flips a pencil lazily
in the air and reads The Orchid Thief.

                    DONALD
          Have you checked out Laroche's porn site?

                    KAUFMAN
          No. I'm trying to read.

                    DONALD
          Anyway, I'm gonna look at the porn site.
          Research.
              (MORE)

                                              (CONTINUED)

CONTINUED:

                    DONALD (CONT'D)
           (chuckles lasciviously)
     Don't tell my old lady.

                    KAUFMAN
     You mean Mom?

                    DONALD
     No, I don't mean Mom. I still say we
     should go to Miami tomorrow.

Donald taps some computer keys.

                    KAUFMAN
     Forget it.

                    DONALD
     Some of these chicks look okay.
     Hey...guess what. We're going to Miami
     tomorrow.

                    KAUFMAN
     I said, no!

                    DONALD
     I said oh, yeah, baby. Come here.

Kaufman sighs, goes over to the computer. On the screen is a
naked photo of Orlean, posed but awkward. Kaufman stares
incredulously at it.

INT. BEDROOM - LATER

Orlean lies in bed with her husband. He sleeps. She stares
up at the ceiling.

                  ORLEAN (VOICE OVER)
     What I came to understand is that change
     is not a choice. Not for a species of
     plant, and not for me. It happens, and
     you are different.

EXT. SWAMP - LATER

The sun is high. Orlean and Laroche sit on dry ground. She
stares at him. He won't look at her, but busies himself
opening the backpack and pulling out food. Finally:

TITLE: FAKAHATCHEE THREE YEARS EARLIER

                  LAROCHE
     You're just like everybody else. Fucking
     leeches. You just attach yourself to me
     and suck --

                                  (CONTINUED)

CONTINUED:

                    ORLEAN (VOICE OVER)
          Maybe the only distinction between the
          plant and me is that afterward --

                    LAROCHE
          ...me dry, spit me out. You know, why
          don't you get your own fuckin' life?
          Your own fuckin' interests? Fuckin' --

                    ORLEAN (VOICE OVER)
          -- I lied about my change. I lied in my
          book. I pretended with my husband that
          everything was the same --

                    LAROCHE
          -- spoiled bitch!

                    ORLEAN (VOICE OVER)
          But something happened in the swamp that
          day.

EXT. SWAMP - DAY

Laroche leads Orlean through the swamp. He spots something
on a tree, circles it, stands there awestruck. Orlean comes
around to see a ghost orchid hanging from the tree.

                    LAROCHE
          Hey, look! I told you I'd find the jewel
          of the Fakahatchee!

Orlean tries to feel some passion, but can't muster it.

                    ORLEAN
          It's a flower. Just a flower.

                    LAROCHE
          Well, might as well grab it. Long as I'm
          here.

Laroche breaks off the branch.

INT. VAN - DAY

Laroche drives. Orlean stares out the window. Laroche tries
to think of something to say.

                    LAROCHE
          Boy, my porn site's gonna be big.

No reaction. They drive in silence. Then:

                                (CONTINUED)

CONTINUED:

                          LAROCHE (CONT'D)
Look, something I didn't tell you. I
want to tell you about the ghost. Okay?
I think it might help you. I'd just
started at the nursery --

Orlean doesn't even acknowledge he's talking.

EXT. SEMINOLE NURSERY TRAILER - NIGHT

Laroche heads up the steps and enters.

                         LAROCHE (VOICE OVER)
-- and I went back one night to pick up
something.

INT. TRAILER BACK ROOM - NIGHT

Laroche peeks in the room. A bunch of young, stoned Indian
men. Some stare off. One sings to himself. Two of the men
make out. One of the men is slicing up a ghost orchid and
pulverizing it. One of the men looks up and sees Laroche.

INT. VAN - DAY

Laroche drives.

                         LAROCHE
They wanted the ghost just to extract the
drug. It had been a ceremonial thing,
but the young guys, you know, they liked
to get stoned.

Orlean seems interested now.

                         ORLEAN
So, Matthew? He was one of the guys --

                         LAROCHE
Sure! Matthew lived on that shit till
they ran out.

                         ORLEAN
Because there was this one day he was...
fascinated by me. By my hair... my
sadness.

                         LAROCHE
Yeah, well, it does that. That's what I
wanted to tell you. I mean, I think
you'd like it, Susie. It seems to help
people be fascinated. Y'know, I can
extract it for you. I know how.
                    (MORE)

CONTINUED:

                    LAROCHE (CONT'D)
      I watched. I'm probably the only white
      guy who knows. I want to do this, Susie.

                    ORLEAN
      I'm done with orchids, Laroche.

INT. HOTEL ROOM - NIGHT

Orlean sits blankly on her bed. There's a package with her
name written on it on the night table. Next to it are some
lines of green powder. She hesitates, then snorts a small
amount, stands, tries to determine if it's going to kill her.
She feels nothing. She snorts the rest, stands again, tries
to feel something, doesn't. She sighs.

INT. HOTEL BATHROOM - A FEW MOMENTS LATER

Orlean brushes her teeth, dully watches herself in the
mirror. Suddenly she becomes fixated on the white suds in
her mouth, on the wonderful sensation of bristles against
gum, on the scrubbing sound. A smile lights her face and
toothpaste dribbles down her chin. She watches her grinning
face with love. She bends in to the mirror for a better
look. She giggles. She alters the rhythm of her brushing.
She makes various shapes with her mouth to change the tone.

INT. HOTEL ROOM - A LITTLE LATER

Orlean lies sprawled on her back on the bed, holding the
phone to her ear, listening to the dial tone. It's so
beautiful. She tries to hum along with it.

Later: The phone rings. A stoned Orlean eventually picks it
up.

                    ORLEAN
          (into telephone)
      Hello?

                    LAROCHE (O.S.)
          (over telephone)
      Hi.

INT. LAROCHE'S BEDROOM - CONTINUOUS

Laroche sits at his desk.

                    LAROCHE
          (into telephone)
      It's John. Did...you get my package?

                    ORLEAN (O.S.)
          (over telephone, excitedly)
      John? John!

CONTINUED:

Laroche smiles.

INT. ORLEAN'S HOTEL ROOM - CONTINUOUS

Orlean lies on her back on the phone.   She plays with the
phone cord.

                    ORLEAN
                (into telephone)
        Johnny...
                (idea)
        Hey, John?

She studies her feet.

                    LAROCHE (O.S.)
                (over telephone)
        Yeah?

                    ORLEAN
        I'm very happy now.

                    LAROCHE (O.S.)
        Well, I'm glad.

INT. LAROCHE'S BEDROOM - CONTINUOUS

                    ORLEAN (O.S.)
                (over telephone)
        ...Um...John?

                    LAROCHE
                (into telephone)
        Hm?

INT. ORLEAN'S HOTEL ROOM - CONTINUOUS

                    ORLEAN
                (into telephone)
        Will you go like this?

Orlean hums the dial tone.   Laroche tries unsuccessfully to
imitate her.   His voice is not good.

                    ORLEAN (CONT'D)
                (into telephone)
        No.   No.

Laroche tries again.   Orlean tries to hum along to create the
dial tone.   Laroche's voice fluctuates wildly.   Orlean bursts
into stoned, hysterical giggles.

(CONTINUED)

CONTINUED:

                    ORLEAN (CONT'D)
I'm trying to make a dial tone. And you
have to sustain...and then I will join
you...and together.... See, I can't do
it by myself.

                    LAROCHE
          (over telephone)
Okay, which one do you want me to do?
          (sings higher tone)

                    ORLEAN
          (into telephone)
Yes! Yes! Yes!

                    LAROCHE
          (over telephone)
Okay. Here we go.
          (sings higher tone)

Orlean sings the lower tone. It works. It's surprisingly
beautiful.

                    ORLEAN
That's it.

                    LAROCHE
          (over telephone)
We got it.

                    ORLEAN
          (into telephone)
We got it. That's fucking amazing.

INT. HOTEL ROOM - MUCH LATER

Orlean is on the floor, on the phone, but not talking. She
stares out the window at the early morning light. Finally:

                    ORLEAN
          (into telephone)
Do you ever get lonely sometimes, Johnny?

                    LAROCHE (O.S.)
          (over telephone)
Well, I was a weird kid...

INT. LAROCHE'S BEDROOM - NIGHT

Laroche lies on his bed and talks on the phone.

                                (CONTINUED)

CONTINUED:

            LAROCHE
      Nobody liked me. I had this idea if I
      waited long enough, someone would come
      around and just, y'know, understand me.
      Like my mom. Except someone else.

INT. VAN - NIGHT

The van is parked on the beach. The back doors are open.
Orlean and Laroche make love inside on a sleeping bag. The
junk is pushed to the sides. Laroche seems clumsy, but
Orlean is enraptured: every touch sends her further into the
experience. She glances past Laroche at the moon. She sees
the moonlight reflecting off the junk in the van. Everything
glows with unearthly beauty: a coke can, a bag of soil, some
lines of the green powder spread on a trowel. Orlean looks
with love at these items, then at Laroche's straining face.
She pulls him to her and kisses him.

            LAROCHE (VOICE OVER)
      She'd look at me and quietly say
      "yes." Just like that. And I wouldn't be
      alone anymore.

EXT. LAROCHE'S BACKYARD - DAY

Laroche is inside a make-shift greenhouse tending to several
immature ghost orchids. Orlean lies on the grass outside,
transfixed by a colony of ants. The sun is warm on her skin.

            ORLEAN
      I wish I were an ant. Oh, they're so
      shiny.

            LAROCHE
      You're shinier than any ant, darlin'.

            ORLEAN
      That's the sweetest thing anybody has
      ever said to me.

            LAROCHE
      I like you, that's why.

                      FADE TO BLACK.

                         FADE IN:

INT. RENTAL CAR - SUNSET

Kaufman and Donald are parked in the loading area at the
Miami Airport, Donald behind the wheel. Orlean waits on the
sidewalk with a suitcase. The beat-up white van pulls up.

                       (CONTINUED)

CONTINUED:

                    DONALD
          Hey.

Orlean gets in, the van speeds off. Donald follows.

INT. CAR - DUSK

Donald drives, keeping up with the van, which speeds and
swerves through traffic. Kaufman is sweaty, nervous.

EXT. SUBURBAN STREET - NIGHT

The van pulls into the driveway of a neat, middle-class
house. Kaufman and Donald drive by, in time to see Orlean
and Laroche emerge from the van. Orlean seems different now:
more exotic. Donald parks up the street, gets out, and
watches as Laroche lugs Orlean's suitcase into the house.

                    DONALD
               (whispering)
          I'll get a closer look. You wait here.

                    KAUFMAN
          No, wait!

Kaufman gets out of the car.

                    KAUFMAN (CONT'D)
          I should go. I mean, it should be me,
          right? I mean, it's my...

                    DONALD
          Go for it, bro. You the man.

Donald gets in, peruses Kaufman's script. Kaufman walks past
the house, trying to peer in windows. He slinks around back.
His eyes widen as he discovers a greenhouse filled with row
upon row of ghost orchids. There's movement in a window in
the house. Kaufman ducks, crawls to the window, looks in.
Orlean and Laroche are laughing, kissing, undressing each
other. Kaufman is heartbroken and transfixed.

                    LAROCHE
          Oh, Darlin', I don't know what's come
          over you.

                    ORLEAN
          You came all over me last time I
          was here, as I recall.

                    LAROCHE
          My goodness.

                                        (CONTINUED)

CONTINUED:

Orlean pulls away giggling, crawls to the coffee table,
snorts some lines of green powder. Laroche waits patiently.
She drags herself back to him and continues where they left
off. Laroche glances at the window, locks eyes with Kaufman

                    LAROCHE (CONT'D)
          I'll be goddamned!

Laroche jumps up and runs naked to the back door. Kaufman
makes a mad dash around the side of the house.

                    LAROCHE (CONT'D)
          Hey, you motherfucker! Hey!

                    KAUFMAN
          Hey!

Laroche cuts him off, drags him into the house.

INT. HOUSE - CONTINUOUS

Laroche throws Kaufman down into a chair.

                    KAUFMAN
          Hey, look-- Wait a minute-- Just-- Why
          don't we just--

                    LAROCHE
          Shut the fuck up now!

Kaufman rises. Orlean rises.

                    ORLEAN
          Who is that, Johnny?

                    LAROCHE
          Who the fuck are you?!

                    KAUFMAN
          I just -- Nobody.

                    LAROCHE
          Huh?!

                    KAUFMAN
          I just-- I'm just--

                    ORLEAN
          Wait a minute.

Orlean studies Kaufman.

                                            (CONTINUED)

CONTINUED:

                    ORLEAN (CONT'D)
          You know who th-- He's that
          screenwriter.

                    LAROCHE
          What, the guy that's adapting our book?

                    ORLEAN
          Yeah.

                    LAROCHE
               (suddenly thrilled)
          Well, that's wild.
               (to Kaufman, shaking his hand)
          It's nice to meet you. Hey, dude, who's
          gonna play me?

                    KAUFMAN
          I'm not-- I don't know that. I should--

                    LAROCHE
          Well, I thought I should play me.

                    ORLEAN
          Did he follow me here?

                    KAUFMAN
          No, of course not. I should go.

                    LAROCHE
          Yeah, yeah. I mean, it was nice to meet
          you. Let me give you my number.

                    ORLEAN
          No. I'm really freaking here, Johnny.
          Why is he here? Why did he follow me?
          What does he know?

                    KAUFMAN
          I don't know anything about anything.

                    LAROCHE
          He did see the greenhouse.

                    ORLEAN
          Oh, shit! Are you gonna write about this
          in your screenplay?

                    KAUFMAN
          I really don't know what "this" is.

Orlean sees Kaufman glance at the drugs on the coffee table.

                                             (CONTINUED)

CONTINUED: (2)

ORLEAN
He's lying. Hold him.

Kaufman gets up. Laroche pushes him back into the chair.

LAROCHE
(shouting at Kaufman)
Stay! Just....

Orlean and Laroche stare at each other. Orlean sits, ponders
for a very long moment.

ORLEAN
(far away)
We have to kill him.

LAROCHE
What?!

ORLEAN
I don't know! What are we supposed to
do? You tell me! What can we do?!

Kaufman tries to stand once more.

LAROCHE
(to Kaufman)
Sit the fuck down!

Kaufman does. Orlean tries to focus.

EXT. RENTAL CAR - CONTINUOUS

Donald gets out of the car

INT. LAROCHE'S HOUSE - CONTINUOUS

LAROCHE
Susie, you got to calm down. You're
getting a little emotional. And, you
don't know what --

ORLEAN
I can't have him writing about me. I
can't have...the whole world -- all the
people knowing about us ... about this.

LAROCHE
Why? You ashamed of me, Susie?

(CONTINUED)

CONTINUED:

                    ORLEAN
        No, that's not it. No! How could you
        even think of that? I'm a professional
        journalist, and the drugs and --

                    LAROCHE
        Susie, we can't kill anyone.

                    ORLEAN
        Okay. Okay. Then I'll do it. By myself.

Kaufman jumps up.

EXT. LAROCHE'S HOUSE - CONTINUOUS

Donald listens outside the window. An offscreen scuffle.

                    LAROCHE (O.S.)
           (shouting at Kaufman)
        Hey!...Come on... get down!

                    ORLEAN (O.S.)
        Put him in his fucking car!

INT. RENTAL CAR - NIGHT

Kaufman drives through a nice, suburban Miami neighborhood.
His headlights shine on Laroche's van ahead. Orlean sits
next to him, holding a gun. She skims Kaufman's screenplay.

Later: They drive through a swampy area, following Laroche's
van past the Fakahatchee Strand State Preserve sign.

EXT. JANES SCENIC DRIVE - A LITTLE WHILE LATER

Laroche's van stops in the middle of the road. His hand out
the window indicates that Kaufman should pull off to the
right onto a logging road. Kaufman does, pulls up to a metal
barrier and parks. Laroche parks behind, blocking him in.

INT. RENTAL CAR - CONTINUOUS

Orlean points the gun at Kaufman

                    ORLEAN
            (to Kaufman)
        Turn it off, and get out.

Kaufman gets out of the car. Orlean does also, keeping the
gun on him. Chime of keys left in ignition

As Kaufman comes around the car to join Orlean, he sees
Donald, wild-eyed, on the floor in the back.

CONTINUED:

Laroche is in the rear of his van, getting some equipment.
As Orlean goes to meet Kaufman, Donald swings open the back
right passenger door, hitting her and sending her flying.

> DONALD
> (to Kaufman)
> Run! Run!

Laroche pokes his head out of the back of his van in time to
see Donald grabbing Kaufman and dragging him into the swamp.

> LAROCHE
> Susan?! What the fuck was that?

> ORLEAN
> I don't know! I couldn't see!

> LAROCHE
> Shit!! fuck!!! Come on. Help me find
> the flashlights.

Orlean pulls herself up and drags herself over to the van as
Laroche is throwing things around in the messy back,
searching for flashlights. We see the lovely Coke can, now
quite plain.

EXT. SWAMP - CONTINUOUS

Kaufman and Donald slog through the black swamp, tripping
over unseen vines. Laroche and Orlean banging around in his
van can be heard in the distance.

Laroche and Orlean have found the flashlights and have
entered the swamp. The beams search the darkness near the
brothers. Donald pulls Kaufman behind a stand of trees.
They sit and wait in silence, breathing hard. Orlean and
Laroche are heard slogging and whispering in the distance.

> LAROCHE
> So it was a guy?

> ORLEAN
> Yeah. Fat. That's all I could tell.

> LAROCHE
> Oh, this is ridiculous. We're gonna have
> to split up.

> ORLEAN
> I'm not gonna be by myself out here.

Orlean and Laroche are very close. Then they move off and
their voices get far away.

(CONTINUED)

CONTINUED:

                    KAUFMAN
They're gonna find us.

                    DONALD
I don't think so.

                    KAUFMAN
I don't want to die, Donald. I've wasted
my life. God, I've wasted it.

                    DONALD
You did not. And you're not gonna die.

                    KAUFMAN
I wasted it. I admire you, Donald, you
know? I spent my whole life paralyzed,
worrying about what people think of me,
and you, you're just oblivious.

                    DONALD
I'm not oblivious.

                    KAUFMAN
No, you don't understand. I mean that as
a compliment. There was this time in high
school. I was watching you out the
library window and you were talking to
Sarah Marsh.

                    DONALD
Oh, God, I was so in love with her.

                    KAUFMAN
I know. And, and you were flirting with
her and she was being really sweet to
you.

                    DONALD
I remember that.

                    KAUFMAN
And then when you walked away she started
making fun of you with Kim Canetti. And
it was like they were, they were laughing
at me. I mean...you didn't know at all.
You seemed so happy.

                    DONALD
I knew. I heard them.

                    KAUFMAN
Well, how come you were so happy?

CONTINUED: (2)

                    DONALD
        I loved Sarah, Charles. It was mine,
        that love. I owned it. Even Sarah
        didn't have the right to take it away. I
        can love whoever I want.

                    KAUFMAN
        But she thought you were pathetic.

                    DONALD
        That was her business, not mine. You are
        what you love, not what loves you.
        That's what I decided a long time ago.

Kaufman and Donald sit there for a long while in silence.
Kaufman starts to cry softly.

                    DONALD (CONT'D)
        What's up?

                    KAUFMAN
        Thank you.

                    DONALD
        For what?

Orlean and Laroche are getting close again. Flashlight beams
miss Kaufman and Donald by inches.

                    ORLEAN (O.S.)
        No...shh, shh, shh, shh! I hear them.
        I hear them. I hear them breathing.
            (calling)
        Charlie? Charlie?

                    LAROCHE (O.S.)
            (calling)
        Charlie?

Overlapping shouts of "Charlie?" fade out. The flashlights
shine elsewhere and the voices go far away.

                                        DISSOLVE TO:

EXT. SWAMP - EARLY MORNING

The light is gray, pre-dawn, murky. Donald and Kaufman are
asleep. Donald awakens, looks around. The rental car is
still there, but there's no van. Donald nudges Kaufman. He
wakes, looks at Donald, who indicates the missing van.

                                        (CONTINUED)

CONTINUED:

> KAUFMAN
> (quietly)
> Where's the van? Is it gone?

> DONALD
> I don't know. Maybe.

They quietly slog toward the road. There's no sign of
Laroche or Orlean. Donald looks back and smiles at Kaufman.
They're getting out of here. Kaufman feels a new, profound
affection for his brother. He pats Donald on the back. It's
an awkward tap, something never attempted before. Donald
gives a cheerful thumbs-up without looking back. They arrive
at the car. Donald is heading around to the passenger side
and stops dead in his tracks. Kaufman looks over to see
what's caught Donald's eye: there, sitting propped against a
tree, sleeps Laroche, his rifle on the ground next to him.
Kaufman and Donald are momentarily frozen. Then:

> ORLEAN
> John? John!

Kaufman and Donald whirl around to see Orlean eyeing them as
she emerges from the van parked up the road.

Laroche opens his eyes. With a groggy start he sees the
identical brothers standing before him. He instinctively
grabs for the rifle. To everyone's surprise it fires.
Donald is hit in the arm. He yelps. Laroche is wide-eyed,
doesn't know what to do. Kaufman grabs Donald and shoves him
in the driver's side door. Kaufman gets in behind him.
Laroche approaches the car. Kaufman starts the car, backs
wildly onto Janes Scenic Drive.

They pass Orlean next to the van. Kaufman and Donald both
crane their necks to watch her recede as they drive the swamp
road.

INT. RENTAL CAR - CONTINUOUS

Kaufman driving. Donald in the midst of an adrenaline rush.

> DONALD
> I can't believe I got shot.
> (laughing)
> Isn't that fucked up?

> KAUFMAN
> (laughing)
> Shut up. Stop laughing.

(CONTINUED)

CONTINUED:

Then, from around a curve, a ranger truck comes barreling.
The two vehicles collide and spin violently around. The
driver's side airbag deploys. Donald flies through the
windshield. Kaufman regains his bearings and sees his
brother halfway out the car, the front of his body a bloody
mess. Kaufman hurries around the car to Donald, who is
conscious, but fading fast. Kaufman tries to keep him awake,
at the same time watching out for Orlean and Laroche.

                    KAUFMAN (CONT'D)
          Donald? You're gonna be okay. It's
          gonna be okay, Donald. Just don't go to
          sleep. Just don't go to sleep, Donald.
          Look at me. Look at me, Donald. Keep
          looking at me. Open your eyes. Donald,
          please open your eyes. Donald, please
          open your eyes, Donald. Donald! Donald,
          open your eyes!

Donald's eyes close. Kaufman starts to sing.

                    KAUFMAN (CONT'D)
          `Imagine me and you, I do...I think about
          you day and night, it's only right to
          think about the one you love and hold her
          tight...So happy together!'
               (speaking)
          Look. Look at me. Look.
               (singing)
          `Imagine me and you, I do...And I--'

Donald is dead.

                    KAUFMAN (CONT'D)
               (shouting)
          Help!

Kaufman looks around spots Orlean watching him. As Kaufman
and Orlean stare at each other, it's obvious to both that
this has gone beyond the point of no return. Kaufman must be
next. He bolts into the swamp. She follows.

                    ORLEAN
          John!

Laroche sees Kaufman running into the woods. He angles in to
cut him off.

EXT. SWAMP - CONTINUOUS

Laroche and Orlean, running from two different directions,
gain on Kaufman and limit his options. Kaufman finds himself
up against a lake. Alligators swim in it.

                                              (CONTINUED)

CONTINUED:

There's nowhere to go. Orlean and Laroche arrive, stop,
heave. The three stare at each other. Finally:

                    LAROCHE
                 (sobbing)
            I'm sorry that I have to do this, dude.
            I'm not a killer. You put yourself in
            our --

Laroche steps on something -- An alligator: it awakens,
startled and angry, and reflexively grabs Laroche's leg. His
rifle fires at nothing. Orlean screams. The alligator
pulls Laroche to the ground and tears him apart. Kaufman
watches. Orlean rushes toward Laroche.

                    ORLEAN
            No...no! Oh, Johnny. Oh, God!

The alligator is gone. Orlean pulls Laroche's body onto dry
land. Kaufman stands on another little island watching for
alligators.

                    ORLEAN (CONT'D)
                 (sobbing)
            Oh, no, no, no...Oh...God. Johnny--
            Johnny-- Johnny--
                 (screaming at Kaufman)
            Oh, you fat piece of shit! He's dead,
            you...

                    KAUFMAN
            Shut up!

                    ORLEAN
            ...loser!

                    KAUFMAN
            Shut up!

                    ORLEAN
            You ruined my life, you...

                    KAUFMAN
            Shut up!

                    ORLEAN
            ...fat fuck!

                    KAUFMAN
            Fuck you, lady! You're just a lonely,
            old desperate, pathetic drug addict!

                                          (CONTINUED)

CONTINUED: (2)

Orlean screams a wordless, wild, tormented, otherworldy
scream. Kaufman just watches, stunned. Then they are
suddenly both silent, heaving.

                    ORLEAN
               (sobbing)
          Oh, my God. It's over. Everything's
          over. I did everything wrong. I want my
          life back. I want it back before it all
          got fucked up. I want to be a baby
          again. I want to be new. I want to be
          new.

Orlean collapses into a heap, sobbing. Kaufman watches,
suddenly feeling so much for this person, this concept turned
flesh before his eyes. The sun is rising. She glows.

EXT. SWAMP - DAWN

Kaufman sits, dazed, on the back of a ranger truck, legs
dangling. Around him there's a flurry of activity.
Ambulance attendants are loading bodies into ambulances,
police are photographing skids on the road, a woman in a
bathrobe is crying and being comforted by a ranger, a tow
truck driver is hooking Kaufman's smashed rental car up to
his truck. The driver pulls some stuff from the car, hauls
it over and places it quietly on the ground next to Kaufman:
some suitcases, Donald's backpack, a copy of Kaufman's
script.

A cop hands Kaufman a cell phone. He dials it.

                    KAUFMAN'S MOTHER (O.S.)
               (over cell phone)
          Hello?... Hello?

                    KAUFMAN
               (sobbing)
          Mom?

                    KAUFMAN'S MOTHER
               (over cell phone)
          Charles? Charles, is that you?...
          Charles, what's the matter? You okay?

Kaufman can only weep.

INT. KAUFMAN'S DINING ROOM - DAY

Kaufman tries to eat his meal, but can't. He looks over at
Donald's empty chair and desk in the living room.

INT. KAUFMAN'S BEDROOM - NIGHT

Kaufman types. The cassette tape recorder is on playback

                KAUFMAN
           (tape recorder voice)
      Donald says, "That was her business, not
      mine. You are what you love, not what
      loves you. I decided that a long time
      ago." Kaufman starts to cry. He tries
      to thank his brother, but he can't put it
      into words.

EXT. SUNSET FIVE PLAZA - DAY

Kaufman sits with Amelia outside the coffee shop. His head
wound has healed.

                AMELIA
      So, how you getting on?

                KAUFMAN
      I'm okay. I miss him, you know.

There is a silence.

                AMELIA
      How's the script coming?

                KAUFMAN
      It's good. I'm almost finished. I'll,
      I'll be really glad to move onto
      something else.

                AMELIA
           (laughs)
      I'll bet.

                KAUFMAN
      Things okay with you?

EXT. ANOTHER PART OF THE PLAZA - A BIT LATER

They walk, look in store windows.

                AMELIA
      ...and then in January, David and I went
      to Prague. That was a high point.

                KAUFMAN
      Sounds great.

                              (CONTINUED)

CONTINUED:

                              AMELIA
              There's amazing puppet theater there!

                              KAUFMAN
              Yeah, I've heard about that. I've always
              wanted to see that.

                              AMELIA
              Yeah, and there's this church decorated
              with, like, human skulls and bones.
              Forty thousand skulls and bones. I
              thought about you when I went there.

Kaufman is touched by this. He kisses her. She kisses him
back, tenderly. Then:

                              AMELIA (CONT'D)
              Charlie, I'm with someone. Why are you
              doing this now?

                              KAUFMAN
              I love you.

                              AMELIA
              I should go. I have stuff I have to do.
              I'm going away this weekend and I have a
              million things, okay?

                              KAUFMAN
              Yeah.

She looks up nervously. He smiles. She smiles back.

                              AMELIA
              I love you, too, y'know.

Amelia hurries off.

INT. PARKING GARAGE - A FEW MINUTES LATER

Kaufman is in his car, waiting to give his ticket to the
attendant so he can leave the garage. He thinks about
something and smiles.

                              KAUFMAN (VOICE OVER)
              I have to go right home. I know how to
              finish the script now. It ends with
              Kaufman driving home after his lunch with
              Amelia, thinking he knows how to finish
              the script. Shit, that's voice over.
              McKee would not approve. How else can I
              show his thoughts? I don't know. Well,
              who cares what McKee says?
                              (MORE)

                                              (CONTINUED)

CONTINUED:

                    KAUFMAN (VOICE OVER) (CONT'D)
It feels right. Conclusive. I wonder
who's gonna play me. Someone not too
fat. I like that Gerard Depardieu, but
can he not do the accent? Anyway, it's
done...and that's something.
So...Kaufman drives off from his
encounter with Amelia, filled for the
first time with hope. I like this. This
is good.

As he heads out of the garage, the film goes to time-lapse
and days and days pass. Morning glories in a planter open
and close with the shifts from day to night.

                                    FADE TO BLACK.

WHITE TEXT ON BLACK SCREEN:

"We're all one thing, Lieutenant. That's what I've come to
realize. Like cells in a body. 'Cept we can't see the body.
The way fish can't see the ocean. And so we envy each other.
Hurt each other. Hate each other. How silly is that? A
heart cell hating a lung cell."

                            - Cassie from The Three

        In Loving Memory of Donald Kaufman

             THE END

STILLS

Twin brothers Charlie, left, and Donald Kaufman *(both played by Nicolas Cage)* on the set of *Being John Malkovich*.

Susan Orlean *(Meryl Streep)*, an esteemed reporter for *The New Yorker*, chats with John Laroche, the protagonist of her book *The Orchid Thief*.

John Laroche *(Chris Cooper)* will go to any length to find rare species of the orchid flower.

Charlie Kaufman *(Nicolas Cage)* attempts to write his latest screenplay, an adaptation of Susan Orlean's *The Orchid Thief.*

Donald *(Nicolas Cage)* and his girlfriend Caroline *(Maggie Gyllenhaal)* at a Hollywood party.

Donald, center, embarrasses Charlie *(both played by Nicolas Cage)* at the party with his antics.

Distressed Charlie Kaufman, right, struggles to balance his screenplay, his life, and his live-in brother Donald *(both played by Nicolas Cage)*.

Charlie *(Nicolas Cage)* tries to confront author Susan Orlean *(Meryl Streep)* in hopes of finding inspiration for his screenplay.

Susan Orlean *(Meryl Streep)* observes John Laroche *(Chris Cooper)* at an orchid show.

Director Spike Jonze, center, talks with actor Nicolas Cage (who plays Charlie Kaufman, seated, and Donald Kaufman, on the ground) on the set of *Adaptation*.

Susan Orlean *(Meryl Streep)* and John Laroche *(Chris Cooper)* bond over a search for the elusive Ghost Orchid.

John Laroche *(Chris Cooper)* tries to find his way out of the Fakahatchee Strand State Preserve.

Susan Orlean *(Meryl Streep)* questions her unexpected emotions.

Charlie Kaufman *(Nicolas Cage)* asks a question at the Robert McKee screenwriting
seminar.

Charlie, left, reads from Robert McKee's *Story* while Donald looks for clues in Susan
Orlean's *The Orchid Thief*.

Donald Kaufman shows Charlie Kaufman *(both played by Nicolas Cage)* the completed draft of his screenplay *The 3*.

Donald left, and Charlie *(both played by Nicolas Cage)* quickly hatch a plan.

Events take a strange turn for John Laroche *(Chris Cooper)*.

The search for the orchid springs forth hidden passions in writer Susan Orlean
(Meryl Streep).

The "real" Robert McKee, left, and Brian Cox (who plays Robert McKee in *Adaptation*).

Charlie Kaufman *(Nicolas Cage)*, left, discusses the structure of his screenplay with screen-writing guru Robert McKee *(Brian Cox)*.

Director Spike Jonze, left, with actor Nicolas Cage

Director Spike Jonze, right, discusses a scene with Nicolas Cage, who plays Charlie Kaufman and Donald Kaufman.

Director Spike Jonze holds a script page from *Adaptation*.

Q & A

WITH CHARLIE KAUFMAN & SPIKE JONZE
BY ROB FELD

To begin with, I had spent the past four days driving and navigating in L.A., which was enough to give an ulcer the size of Vesuvius to any New York boy who learned his L.A. traffic laws from lines in *Annie Hall*. (Stopped at my first red light, Woody's voice came unto me like Obi-Wan's, and I made a California right turn.) What was worse, I realized while swerving across three lanes so as not to miss my turnoff onto Pico—my belated apologies to that red Jaguar—was that soon I'd be returning to New York, where it would be my duty to write an article that might shed some light onto the work of Charlie Kaufman and Spike Jonze—a duo whose reputations for interview lockjaw had acquired mythic status.

Extensive research had nearly brought on paralysis. The more I dug, the more knotted my stomach became. In what is put forth as the director's interview on the *Being John Malkovich* DVD, Jonze suddenly vomits, rather than answer questions. Kaufman, in a panel discussion during the WGAw Words Into Pictures convention, deferred frequently to Jonze and responded with a number of "I don't know's" to questions that tried to label things too precisely.

What truly had me diving for the Maalox, though, was the published *Human Nature* shooting script (Newmarket Press), boasting a Q&A with Kaufman, which was, in fact, written entirely *by* him, *as* him, but in the *voice* of writer/director P. T. Anderson (*Magnolia, Boogie Nights*). Kaufman begins the published interview by mentioning his girlfriend,

---

Rob Feld is a filmmaker who writes on film for a variety of sources. His industry analysis, essays, and interviews appear frequently in the Writers Guild of America monthly magazine, *Written By*.

Mercedes Ruehl (whom I would bet good money he has never met), ends by questioning himself about scenes in *Magnolia* as though they were in *Human Nature*, and precedes the whole thing with a photograph which is of anybody *but* him.

I had committed to 80 minutes in a sealed room with the pair, and I was nursing a nagging fear that I would be returning to New York with a tape full of deflected questions, outright lies, and long silences broken only by the occasional *Pffttthhh!* of a whoopee cushion. I was having trouble reconciling this image of them with the work they did, however. Lore of Kaufman's paralyzing shyness and Jonze's frenetic inability to carry on a conversation sounded slightly like legends of dragons and hobgoblins to me. After all, these were two craftsmen, in the most collaborative of mediums, who had successfully communicated to each other and to their crews a myriad of complex and coherent ideas, which had executed, thus far, two films with artistry and aesthetic cohesion.

Nevertheless, as I gratefully ditched my car in a Sony lot (neglecting to note where I parked it, of course), their own publicists were wishing me good luck. I didn't get it. Could they really be the idiot savant freak shows I had been led to believe, or was there a better explanation?

Fearing that trying to dramatize Kaufman might be like trying to dramatize an orchid, I saw myself being forced to enter my story like Kaufman did *Adaptation*, the whole ugly episode ending inevitably with Kaufman and Jonze chasing me with shotguns through the Pirates of the Caribbean exhibit at Disney World. My stomach churning bile, I kicked an assistant off her computer and hurriedly typed, organized, and re-organized my questions in preparation for 80 minutes of well ordered "I don't know's," coughs, and "Umm's."

For all the lip service paid to the idea of film as a collaborative medium, Charlie Kaufman and Spike Jonze are two artists who seem to get it, and thrive as a result, though in so many ways they could not possibly seem more different as individuals. (Jonze reportedly wanted to be a stunt man as a child and has a penchant for irreverent exhibitionism—reference his performance in the Fatboy Slim video he also directed, "Praise You"—and Kaufman would probably rather burst into dust than be forced to bust a move as Jonze did with a trumped-up Torrance Community Dance Group in front of a Westwood movie theater.) But in many, perhaps more substantial, ways they are kindred spirits, sharing similar concerns and tendencies in the work they do both together and apart. Though largely handled differently in their individual output, one theme in particular stands out and makes their work markedly distinctive: empathy for the inner freak.

Jonze's subjects tend to own their freakishness (albeit, many of them have been rock stars), which is a quality that, in Jonze's world, often makes them trendsetters pushing the edge of cool, much like himself. Kaufman's subjects, on the other hand, are self-loathing, uncharismatic, and solitary. His characters are invariably outsiders looking in, tortured by frustration and obscurity, haunted by personal ghosts and obsessions; and to make matters worse, many can't even get laid.

Overflowing with pained specimens of humanity, *Being John Malkovich* is a surrealist farce in which most of the characters want to be anything but what they are....well, not anything: They want to *be* John Malkovich. The actor, known for his eccentric style, is set up as metaphor for all that we want in life but belongs to someone else. Importantly, though, he is a celebrity, albeit a particular type of one, which is the vessel through which so many people in the modern United States evaluate the world. Experiencing and interpreting life through a filter, especially through one of celebrity, is an important theme for both Kaufman and Jonze. They both seem concerned with the growing distance between us and a visceral, organic experience of life, which has become so programmed and formulaically represented by all-pervasive media that our very expectations of life become transmogrified. The freak, as the outsider who just can't fit into this world, plays a crucial and empathetic role in breaking through the false precepts of this new reality in order to find authentic experience. For an audience fed on the endlessly replicated, cookie-cutter stories and two-dimensional characters of modern media culture, this may be a reason why Kaufman and Jonze's alienated characters resonate so widely and well within the latest wave of counterculture—albeit a highly entrenched, commercialized one.

Human Nature continued Kaufman's funhouse-mirror reflection of society, sending up the notion that there's a utopian world someplace other than wherever one is. Utopia isn't in a state of nature, it isn't in society. The best that can be hoped for by Kaufman's fringe characters (which include a 30-something-year-old virgin with the smallest penis in the world, a man raised in the wilderness *as* an ape by a man who *thinks* he's an ape, and a woman suffering from a condition that covers her body in hair) is contentment with where and who they are. Reality may not always be pleasant, but it is *real*, an attribute put at a high premium in a Kaufman script, where lines between reality and fantasy blur. *Human Nature* was produced by Jonze but directed by Michel Gondry.

Kaufman's mind seems to rebel at every point against following the straight line. As a project, Kaufman's third produced film, *Adaptation*, began innocuously enough. Susan Orlean's book *The Orchid Thief* had been optioned to be adapted for the screen. Things got interesting, however, when Kaufman was the writer hired to do the adaptation. The resulting film was to be Kaufman and Jonze's follow up to their collaboration on *Being John Malkovich*, different in so many ways, but just as playful and inventive as their first.

Based on her reporting for *The New Yorker*, the book describes Orlean's experience with a Florida man, John Laroche, who had been arrested for poaching rare orchids from preservation swamplands. Accepting the job while *Being John Malkovich* was going into production, Kaufman soon found himself with a dilemma: How the hell does one dramatize a flower? The advance check had been cashed though, and a script was expected from him. After numerous false starts, Kaufman's solution was to insert into Orlean's true story a fictionalized character named Charlie Kaufman, who happens to be a screenwriter hired to adapt *The Orchid Thief.* To complicate matters further, Kaufman the screenwriter added a twin brother for Charlie named Donald, plus screenplay-structure guru Robert McKee. Continuing his probing meditations on love, Kaufman's script again finds itself seamlessly leaving reality until the audience finds *itself* watching Charlie (Nicolas Cage) and Donald (Cage again) in a deadly cat and mouse chase through the swamp, fleeing a murderous, hopped-up, and armed Susan Orlean (Meryl Streep). And yet the story is still about a flower.

"You are what you love" is the ending ethic of the story, but that, too, arrives with hooks attached. In a state of love, the self can disintegrate, as characters take on each other's creative *and* destructive qualities. The film is beautifully layered, without question a Charlie Kaufman script, described by *New York Times* writer Lyn Hershberg as "wildly self-conscious while at the same time inching toward some post-ironic point of observation. Both sincere and achingly aware of the limitations of sincerity, knowing yet engaged, the script and its hyperaware author could not be more out of the Hollywood mainstream, nor more of the moment."

I trust I gave nothing away there.

My questions typed and put into

some semblance of order, I was finally led into the greenroom, braced to find two impossibly incoherent autistics. What I found, in fact, was a pair of gracious and articulate filmmakers, acutely aware of the truth that there are more questions than answers. Kaufman was, indeed, shy (though slight and with a full head of wild hair—nothing like the overweight and balding Nicolas Cage in *Adaptation*), and one could tell that Jonze likes a joke. Our first five minutes together were spent purposely on speakerphone hold with Jonze's post-production facility, listening to their recording of an hysterical series of faux Italian lessons taken from the ridiculous things commonly heard in an editing suite, followed by Italian translation: "We could make it look like Paris," "Good ideas come from anywhere," "Have you ever seen the movie *Brazil*?"

Both seemed concerned with the idea of representation; of signs and signifiers and how we read and experience them—I couldn't help but connect that Kaufman is reluctant to have publicity photos taken, and Mrs. Spiegel did not name her baby boy "Spike." In *Human Nature*, two of Kaufman's characters abandon the use of language altogether because—no matter how earnestly employed—words can only approximate the truth, and therefore lead only to more lies. *Malkovich* deals primarily with the way many experience life: through the synthetic filter of somebody else's experience. Though *Human Nature* is tongue-in-cheek about the myth of a purity found in the wild, both it and *Malkovich* dismantle the artificiality of societal constructs; *Adaptation* is about a writer who becomes fixated on the woman whose experience he's trying to represent in his writing. If the medium is the message, and the concerns of Truth are in the foremost of one's mind, one must choose words with care and, of equal importance, economy.

```
EXT. FOREST — NIGHT

Puff and Lila have built a makeshift shelter out of
leaves and twigs. They are sitting around a campfire,
naked and dirty, roasting a couple of skinned
squirrels on sticks. The black box rests on Lila's
lap. Puff looks at the roasting squirrel, is repulsed.
```

```
                    PUFF
        Nice Night.


                    LILA
        Language was invented so people could
        lie to each other and themselves.

Puff begins to disagree. Lila's hand hovers over the
button. He stops himself.

                    PUFF
                 (confused)
        I agree?


Lila shocks Puff.

                    LILA
        Any answer is the wrong answer.
```

—Charlie Kaufman's *Human Nature*

Why are lesbian separatists so funny? You've put them in two scripts.
Charlie Kaufman: Have I? They've never made it in the movie, though....
I hate when I repeat myself.

You two are known to collaborate very closely.
Spike Jonze: Definitely. All throughout the process. After I read the
script and we start talking about it, then in pre-production and casting—
and production, as much as is possible—and then post-production, definitely.
Both movies, but *Adaptation* more so, I think, because it continued to
evolve a lot in editorial. Charlie and Eric, our editor [film editor Eric
Zumbrunnen who worked on *Malkovich* and *Adaptation*], and I end up working as closely as we can.

Charlie, do you come to the set?
Charlie: As much as I can, but I'm usually working on something else at
the time. There's not much for me to do there.
Spike: I think in important scenes—

Charlie: Yeah, sometimes they'll ask me to be there because there might be a problem, or something we haven't worked out exactly.

Spike: Or a scene we might want to see how it plays and adjust. But, for the most part in production, he'd just be sitting around the lot, so we tend to make it important for him.

***Did you involve Spike while you wrote* Adaptation?**
Charlie: While I was writing this, he was shooting *Malkovich*, so no.
Spike: I didn't mean to say he "sits around," like he's not doing stuff. Did I?
Charlie: No.
Spike: It's just that, unless there's something specific we want him to do...
Charlie: Get coffee, or that kind of thing...So, I was writing this during *Malkovich*, and Spike wasn't originally going to direct it. I was writing it for Jonathan Demme's company. Spike knew about it, because I talked to him about it a lot during *Malkovich*, and then asked if he could direct it, and they said, "Yes."

As you've collaborated on three projects now [Spike produced on* Human Nature*], are there common themes you each find yourselves gravitating towards, or that you find yourselves accentuating as you execute the material?
[Dead silence. Finally, laughter.]
Charlie: I don't know....Apparently I like to write about lesbian separatists. Other than that, I don't have a clue. I've been told I like to write about monkeys, too. So, you know, I don't know. *[Groan]* I don't know. That's the kind of thing that I wish somebody else would answer for me. I try to keep it at kind of a base level and not be too intellectual about it when I write. I try to find where my interests lie and just, sort of, go there.

Where do you usually start?
Charlie: It depends. Sometimes it's an event, sometimes it's more thematic. In this case it was with a book. With *Malkovich,* it was an idea about somebody falling in love with someone who isn't his wife—that was the original idea. I like to feel free. I don't want to know too much when I start. I want to be free to go with it where it takes me.

You said once that you write to surprise yourself.
Charlie: Yeah, that's true. That's a good one. I'm glad I said that. Yeah, I

do. That's important. It energizes the writing. You feel like, "Oh! That's something I want to see, or something I never would have thought of." *[Laughter]*

You guys play with structure a good deal. You don't outline, do you?
Charlie: No, I don't like to. I mean, I've done it. I've worked in TV a lot, so...

What is the central thing, do you think, then, that keeps the whole story together and lets you be so flexible with structure?
Charlie: In any case, or in the case of *Adaptation*?

Either/or.
Charlie: You know, I should clarify that when I say I don't outline or structure, it doesn't mean that I just write it in one draft and then it gets made into a movie. I go back, I change things, I figure out something that happens *here* that interests me that I need to set up *here*, which is earlier in the script. So, hopefully, there ultimately starts to be some kind of structure. I just don't want to draw an outline and then color it in because it doesn't interest me and I don't find anything that way. Then I go back and I try to structure. You know, I'm interested in *things*. I'm interested in people and how they interact and, if I ever do it well, then it's interesting. It's not about FX or pyrotechnics or a string of gags for me—even though I like stuff like that—I'm more interested in the people there.

Do you think it's a strong character or character relationships that then keep you on solid ground?
Charlie: Either character relationships or someone's relationship with him- or herself. I mean, how you are in the world, how you're not in the world. But, yeah.

So, it develops in layers then.
Charlie: Yeah, I would say that's a good way to characterize it.
Spike: I think, also, a big part of why is that—it's not even a first draft—but you end up writing something really long....
Charlie: At times, yeah. With *Adaptation,* it was very long.
Spike: Which is part of him writing what he wants to write, and then being able to go back and look at it.

Charlie: Yeah, I don't like to edit myself while I'm writing—which requires that I do it later.

Like you said, does that make it too intellectual?
Charlie: I just think I find things, you know? If I have a scene, a dialogue between two characters that runs on for five pages, I might find three lines of really good dialogue four pages in, but I wouldn't have found them, and I can just cut out the rest. I can't just go, "So, this has to be a page long, so the page breaks here...." I can't do it like that.

What was your initial reaction to **The Orchid Thief?**
Charlie: I liked it very much—I wanted to adapt it. It seemed not to be a movie, which intrigued me. I liked the book and it wasn't the kind of thing that I was being sent—I was getting sent the weird stuff because *I'm the weirdo.* But, this was a straightforward book—very well written. I was learning things; it was about flowers—there was very little drama in it. It seemed, "Well, it's interesting as a book, why can't it be interesting as a movie?" That was what I initially thought, and then I realized, well, it probably could have been, but not if I wrote it.

You **did** *find a way to dramatize the idea of the flower though.*
Charlie: I hope so.

Do you know how?
Charlie: I don't know. I spent a lot of time on it. The movie's pretty accurate in its depiction of my false starts and my confusion, and how I just had to plug away because I was hired and because they had paid me a certain amount of money to proceed, and so I had to. I would have dropped it a hundred times if they didn't give me that advance money, but I felt obligation. And then, I think, Spike's collaboration brought a lot of it. A lot of how the movie looks now probably came about in editing, working with Spike.

Do you know what the device was that manages to dramatize that flower?
[Long silence]
Charlie: Maybe I do, but I'd rather not say....if that's okay.

One of you once said that you were pretty sure from the beginning that the film would come together in post.

Spike: I can't remember saying that, but we definitely talked about it. I definitely knew that this was going to be a complicated editorial because we were trying to make so many disparate ideas, characters, and moments come together. I think from the get-go we went in knowing that, but I don't think we thought it was going to be as hard as it was. The intention of the script never changed, but how it's come together and how the sequences and scenes fit together—from just basic stuff: how much you intercut, or when you intercut between the multiple characters, where things happen in the story—there was a lot of flexibility. It was like a draft as opposed to our first movie, which did take a while to edit, but involved refining a few things that weren't clear, figuring out pacing and where we wanted to take time or not. This was much more like drafts, which Charlie was rewriting.

Are the scenes in a very different order than in the original script?

Spike: I think if you look at them page by page, but I think if you read the script and watched the movie, I don't think you'd know that they'd been rearranged that much. It was a little like editing a documentary because it could go together in a lot of different ways. It's sort of abstract in that way, where the plot doesn't decide when a scene should go. It left options open so much more.

Did you find yourselves saying, "We need to accentuate this, or we need to..."

Spike: Yeah, and because there were so many different story lines or through lines (Charlie and his writing process, Charlie and his relationship with Amelia, Charlie and his relationship with the book, with Susan Orlean, with Donald, and with Susan Orlean and her relationship with her husband, and with Laroche; and then there's the Ghost Orchid and what it is to Charlie and to Susan and to John Laroche)...So, for a month or two you're focusing on one thing, and you step back and that's starting to work, but then you realize how much something else isn't working. When we showed the movie to Meryl Streep, she called attention to something that was always in the script—but at that point in the editorial process had sort of slipped away—and that was Charlie's...not *obsession* with Susan Orlean...

Charlie: Fixation?

Spike: Fixation and interest in Susan Orlean's writing. And that was something that was in the script and was part of the shoot, but at this point in editorial had sort of faded into the background. So, she brought our attention to it and we were able to focus on that.

Charlie: There were so many things to juggle and think about.

Spike: And *over*think about. You end up overcompensating when something is missing. You go back to the script and put in five moments where he's fixating on her writing, and then it's too many, and then you go back.

There are so many thematic lines in your writing, Charlie, that seem so disparate, but in the end tie up into a whole.

Charlie: I think there are just fortuitous accidents, or something else is going on that I'm unaware of, but I do go back and I do realize that this theme is coming to the fore, and so I'll get excited about that and pull that out. Or, I'll come up with an idea that ties these two stories together and I'll do *that*. It's a bit scary and fun for that reason because I don't know how it's going to end. It helps me keep going.

You used voice-over this time. Was that a device you found necessary to tie it together? Would you use it again? I know it means it can keep changing in post.

Charlie: I wouldn't rule it out. I like voice-over. I like it a lot. You're not supposed to anymore, but I do. It's hard, sometimes, when you're doing very internal pieces. Some movies don't operate that way. Plus, I like the idea of having different types of voice-over—voice-over that's representative of Charlie's writing and then the voice-over that's the inside of Charlie's head. The clash of those two things interests me.

And you gave it a whiz-bang ending.
[General chuckling]

Charlie: Yes, definitely. Always do that. Gotta wow 'em in the end. It's what we learn from McKee.

You've written for both TV and film. Do you find a difference between them? Was one more liberating than the other? Would you do TV again?

Charlie: I would do television again, sure. I wrote for sit-coms, which, I think, are different than one-hour format, from what I've heard. I think there's less of a room, and people write more individually. For sit-com, you're in a room of nine or ten other people, so it's communal writing, and it's pitching jokes and it's competing. You know, it's competitive that way, and I think that, to me—and I had some good experiences—it's much less personal. I couldn't do the stuff that I want to do. I tried. I tried to write some stuff for television that will just never see the light of day. And then this opportunity came along and it seemed much more liberating.

What was the first stuff you started writing? Did you write prose or theater?

Charlie: I wrote plays and I wrote prose and I wrote film stuff for myself. No poetry.

Would you do prose again?

Charlie: Yeah, and I'd like to do a play. I don't really have the time now....

I think you said once that you like to think about why something is funny or terrifying to you, and that's why you write.

Charlie: Yeah, I think you changed the words a bit. I think what I might have said is that I like to write about things that I find funny or terrifying, or a whole bunch of other things. In other words, I try to find some sort of visceral reaction—that's what kind of inspires me. I feel like *my* reaction is the barometer I need to proceed. You know? What else do I have to write about than the things that scare me or fascinate me?

Much of what you're done entails characters defining their own world and experience. Perception is everything. You've got Puff, who's raised by a man who thinks he's an ape (so he might as well be), and in Adaptation, *Donald has a speech about owning his love, which is what defines him. He is what he loves. As a theme or concept—the idea of perception as reality—is that something you find yourself conscious of working with?*

Charlie: I guess, in the sense that I'm aware that I'm in my own head and that's the only thing that I know. Everything else is kind of speculation. I guess, in that sense, then perception is reality...and also your prison. So, yes.

Lynn Hershberg at **The New York Times**...[nervous laughter all around]...*wrote that the "central conflict in [your] writing is the push and pull of reality and the hope provided by fantasy." I wanted to get your feelings on* *that, and I was wondering if it would be hope provided by* **fantasy** *or hope provided by* **perception?**

Charlie: I don't know....Spike and I have long discussions about this—how to talk about the movies—and I think we both agree that we like people to have their interpretations and experiences of the movies, and I don't want to say Lynn Hershberg is right or wrong. I assume Lynn Hershberg is right because that's her take on it. I try to write things so that there's an opportunity to have various experiences. I don't want to dictate anything. It would be really great for different people to have different experiences, or even for the same person to have different experiences at different times. That's my goal. If I could accomplish that I would feel like I was doing well. To say that my movie was about searching for hope, or not searching for hope...I'd rather not.

But, I think the question is more, "What intrigues you about it?" What are you following? People are going to have their experiences of the film no matter what.

Charlie: Right, but if I were to say, "Yes, Lynn Hershberg is right," whatever you told me she said—finding hope through fantasy, is that what she said? If I were to say, "Yes, then you go watch the movie," and you're like "It's about finding hope through fantasy, okay. Gotta go home and get drunk." You know? I don't know. Because I don't put it into words like that for myself, which isn't to say that Lynn Hershberg is wrong—and I'm *not* saying that—but I intentionally, for my own benefit, don't put it into an encapsulated form like that. I always said that one of the things I thought about my writing is that I try to write in the midst of confusion and be strong enough to stay there, rather than swim to the shore of some kind of conclusion, because I think that's how I live my life and to me there's a value in that. There's a value in depicting that and letting people sort of...Since we're in a world of confusion there's lots of different ways to interpret it. That's my experience of life. How was that? Was that bad?

Spike: No.

No, that was great. Thank you.
[General laughter]
Spike: Incredibly articulate.

You've worked with surrealism to some extent, in Malkovich, at any rate, and there's elements of it in other scripts…is there something more real in the surreal? What is it you relate to? What does an audience get from it?

Charlie: I don't know. I like stuff like that. It makes me laugh but it also makes me nervous, and it's kind of dreamlike, so it has that kind of quality to it.…I'm really drawn to it. I don't know why. *[To Spike]* Do you know why?

Do you use surrealism as a tool?

Spike: I'm not sure. It's so much harder to look at something from this vantage point three years later. It's much different from looking at it when you're doing it or trying to figure out how to make it work, or what's interesting or makes sense. What it's about at that moment is so different from what it's about right now. And I think that sort of ties into what Charlie's saying: What a scene is about while we're trying to figure it out—while we're talking about it or trying to shoot it or edit it—part of it always stays the same, part of it changes and also, hopefully, as Charlie was saying, part of it changes from person to person.

You have used many elements of reality, or real people, in your fictional or fictionalized stories—you've got John Malkovich, Charlie Sheen, Robert McKee, Susan Orlean, the list goes on—what effect do you find that having? What do think that does to an audience?

Charlie: Again, just on a visceral level, I think it's funny. Not always, but, in the case of Malkovich, it just struck me as really funny. I can analyze it afterwards and figure out why and what effect it has, but I think that what it does (and in the case of *Adaptation*, especially)…I'm always trying to figure out a way to take a movie from here, out in front of you *[Charlie frames something out in front of him],* and put it *here [he pulls his hands back even with his head].* And I don't know that I'm successful, but it's the way that I thought of it for this one. Take real people, and take the person who really wrote it, and make them characters, and have the experience of watching them write it *be* the experience that the moviegoer has. So, you're constantly being taken out of the movie. Even though you're watching the movie as a story that plays as a story, there's this constant nagging thing that's, "Is this real, is this not real?" I really like that. I don't know why I like it. In theory, it's the difference between a beautiful illustration and a really good painting. One you can look at and enjoy and marvel at the work, and the other just hits you in the face. There's something about movies that's very safe because they usually play out in a certain way, and also because they're *done*. They're *dead*. It's not like theater where anything can happen, where somebody can screw up their lines, or there can be some kind of new interaction or chemistry between people. It's just this dead thing that you're watching, and I don't like that about it. So, if you force people to interact with the movie in a new way, then you're forcing them to see different things and their minds to interact. In a way, that's closer than just sitting back and going, "There's that high speed chase, now." Or, maybe it's just sort of a lack of imagination on my part that I can't write those other kind of things.

I don't think anyone'll every accuse you of a lack of imagination.
Charlie: No, but sometimes it's like, why shouldn't I do just a simple little movie? And I love movies like that when they're good, like someone wrote just great dialogue and great characters and you fall in love with them. In no way am I dismissing those, but maybe it's just not what I can do. *[To Spike]* I feel like every time I talk for a long period of time I have to look at you to see if I made any sense at all, because I have no idea.

Spike: Well, some of your favorite movies…Charlie just told me to see *What Happened Was*. It's interesting because it is a movie about two people on a date that takes place in one night, and the dialogue's incredible and the acting's incredible and the drama all takes place in this apartment and it's really well done. I know Charlie is interested in that….

Charlie: But it's also amazingly well written and acted, and what's so great about the way that movie works—and the way I would hope something that I do might work some day—is that you can watch this very simple movie between two characters and, depending on your mood, see different things in it every time. I think that they workshopped that movie, so I think the subtleties of that movie, of the characterizations, of the dialogue, sort of evolved and evolved—at least, that's sort of what I'm imagining—until it's, like, perfect. Perfect.

One reason why, for me, you two augment each other so well is that, Spike, you very much let the material be and speak for itself. Especially for someone who comes out of music video, you're not doing everything with the camera we know you're capable of. I think everything you do serves what Charlie's written.
Spike: Well…thanks!

Charlie: It's true. He's not showing off, and everything he does is in service of the movie, but I think one of the things that's really quiet and amazing is the work he does with the actors. It's not like he's "letting it happen." He's finding and directing those performances. Everything, to me, is just watching, you know, *real people*, which I think is a very difficult thing to accomplish. I think, in some ways, most of us don't even know what real people act like anymore because we're so used to seeing what movie people act like.

You also said something once about never writing people you don't like, and putting ordinary people in extraordinary circumstances.

Charlie: I remember the first part....I wouldn't put it that way now. I don't know if they're regular people in extraordinary circumstances, but I don't care if they're likable to an audience, but I do want them to be understandable. So, if they're doing something that's extraordinary or unusual, I want that to be what the character is. I just don't think that I write regular people because I don't know what a regular person is. For me to say that would be a lie.

Would you say that every story is about what it is to be human? Or is it all just about getting laid...or is there a difference?

Charlie: You asked me a real question and then you gave me a snappy answer, and now I feel like I have to respond snappily.

Sorry. Please don't.

Charlie: I don't know what else there is to write about other than being human, or, more specifically, being *this* human. I have no alternative. Everything is about that, right? Unless it's about flowers.

Which, at the end of the day, turned out to be about what it was to be human.

Charlie: [*Smiling*] That's right.

CRITICAL COMMENTARY

BY ROBERT McKEE

Charlie Kaufman is an old-fashioned Modernist. He writes in the palaeo-*avant-garde* tradition that runs from the dream plays of Strindberg and inner monologues of Proust through the tortured identities in Pirandello and the paranoia of Kafka to the rush of subjectivities in Wolfe, Joyce, Faulkner, Beckett, and Bergman—that grand twentieth-century preoccupation with the Self.

I'm sure Kaufman's embarrassed to be cited alongside these masters. And he hates being labeled. Who doesn't? But like William Goldman, he's stepped out of screenwriting anonymity to gain national recognition as an artist— without becoming a director. More, unlike Goldman, he's done it while swimming against the commercial current. No small task. So I applaud him, and as I try to place his work in the universe of story, it seems to me that although he may use the disorienting techniques of Postmodernism, he draws upon an older, deeper creed. When he plays with randomness and unreliable realities, when he springs the fantasized into the secular, when he fragments time and place, he doesn't use these devices to express Postmodernism's indifference to the serious or its facetious scorning of sense and values. No, Kaufman, amazingly, like the luminaries of the Modern, still believes that story has meaning.

Adaptation is the thematic sequel to *Being John Malkovich*. In *Malkovich*, characters suffer a claustrophobia of identity. Suffocating in their own skins, weary

---

Robert McKee joined the faculty of the School of Cinema and Television at the University of Southern California (USC) in 1983, where he began offering his now famous "Story Seminar" class. In January of 2000, McKee won the prestigious 1999 International Moving Image Book Award for his bestselling book *Story: Substance, Structure, Style, and the Principles of Screenwriting.*

of an ineffable emptiness, they want to transform. The protagonist, at first, hides behind his puppets. But it's not enough. The answer? Become John Malkovich. What better escape than into a really cool guy who stars in Art Movies, no less? The film was a delight that expressed our bittersweet wish to be somebody else. But a wish is, of course, only that, a wish.

In *Adaptation*, Kaufman abandoned the whimsy of transformation to confront suffering at its source—the war within. He shifted the setting from an alienated social landscape to an innerscape he knows only too well, his own mind.

With the release of *Adaptation* the press tried to stir up that now familiar, and I must say boring, controversy about the ethical use of actual people in fiction. Journalists believe that the truth is what *is*, and so they fumed, "How dare Kaufman portray Susan Orlean as a violent, drug-crazed murderess? My God, she's a journalist for *The New Yorker* magazine!" Truth, however, is not what is, but what we *think about* what is. We who were portrayed realized from scratch that none of us were, in any real sense, actually in the film. Kaufman was after something else, not fact, not us. We were amused—if not disappointed—to discover we'd been hijacked and epitomized to play various roles in the chaotic drama of Kaufman's psychic life.

I well remember that as I read his first draft I was shocked. Beneath the witty wildness, I found a telling, indeed a confession, of nearly shameful intimacy. And by that I don't mean the masturbation scenes. Jerking off in movies is no more embarrassing than smoking. In L.A. nowadays if you really want to suffer chagrin, put a cigarette in your mouth. No, I mean that his pages read like a filmic stream of consciousness, an allegory starring the contentious facets of Kaufman's psyche. He'd given each faction a characterization taken from so-called reality, then declared war on himself. I thought, "This man's been through analysis and it hasn't worked, so now he's dissecting his neuroses in public. He's either got a death wish or the guts of a cat burglar."

Creative conflicts aside, Kaufman is not, apparently, a big fan of Kaufman. So, echoing *Malkovich,* he cast Susan Orlean to portray his self-loathing as she gives a heartbreaking voice to his hunger to transform. And I'm sure that like us all, Kaufman, in his life-long pursuit of inner peace, has tried on one role after another without success. John Laroche, therefore, became the perfect player for that foible, as he constantly reinvents himself, animating each incarnation with magnificent enthusiasm followed by disaster.

Finally, there's McKee. It's no secret that Kaufman hates authority. Who doesn't? But for him it goes a little deeper than most. In his hands I, too, became just a symbol, an icon for that huge, terrifying authority that haunts Kaufman night and day—his Super-ego, his nagging conscience.

The Orchid Thief is Susan Orlean's self-inquisition, a deeply subjective auto-biography cum biography in which she puts herself on the rack for her seeming lack of passion. What's more, it's a *book*. And in it, Orlean does what the prose writer does best: She dramatizes the invisible, the tides and times of inner conflict. But you can't drive a camera lens through an actor's forehead and photograph thought, although there are directors who would try. So *The Orchid Thief* could not be adapted; it had to be reinvented. But as what? Taking a cue from Orlean, Kaufman decided to layer his self-inquisition over her self-inquisition.

But how to do that? Worse, how to do it on screen? The guiding impulse in Kaufman values freedom over restraint, the unusual over the usual. He wants to push the cinema against the grain into hidden humanity, to take it through the frayed synapses of the mind, complete with spiraling free associations and compulsive, self-critical repetitions. The danger, however, is that the film will blur into fragmentary sensations, shadowy simulacra, a random swirl of images that lack depth, coherence, authenticity, and meaning. Indeed, the work may become so personal, so idiosyncratic that no one will know what the hell he's talking about, and therefore, no audience will feel what he feels. And he knows that. He knows that difference for the sake of difference is an empty achievement that expresses nothing but vanity. For at the heart of Kaufman is that dreaded voice of authority, his artist's conscience telling him that like it or not, one way or another, he has to tell the story.

And he did. The overall structure Kaufman created to shape his unruly content counterpoints and then crisscrosses a Disillusionment Plot with an Education Plot, two genres far more typical of a novel than a film, both running inside the mind of the central characters. A Disillusionment Plot opens with a protagonist at the positive, someone with an optimistic view of the world, then arcs him/her to a defeated, pessimistic end. An Education Plot is the opposite. It begins with the protagonist at the negative, clinging to a dark, pessimistic mind-set. Experience then teaches this character to see life anew, arcing him/her to an upbeat, if not optimistic, sense of world and self. The former is Susan's story, the latter, Charlie's. *Adaptation* is a unique and beautifully interlocked figure in which two stories dance together, reinforcing each other, creating an ironic climax to an outrageous work. Orlean is lost, but Charlie is found. He's finished his task, at peace with himself—at least for now.

Despite his ingenious design, Kaufman must have felt that his manic meanderings might alienate the audience. At some point the audience might be thinking, "Man, this is so bizarre none of it makes sense, and why should I give a damn about this Charlie character anyway?" But Kaufman understands deconstructive rhetoric. He knows that we know film is ritual. To involve ourselves we must accept the conventions of the art. If you want to spoil your pleasure, just be that mean-spirited literalist who whines, "But that's not real." So we'll give the writer his/her premise, no matter how wild, just don't insult us. Don't hide your faults, admit them. From the opening scenes we sense Kaufman lurking behind the screen, whispering, "Look, you and I get that this is an exhibitionistic exercise of my angst. Are you with me or not?" And we answer, "Fine, the whole thing's in the head of a self-hating perfectionist. I've been there. On with the movie."

Here's how it works: When Charlie berates himself as a pathetic loser, it prompts us to think: "No, you're not. You only imagine you are. You're really rather lovable." When Charlie swears that there'll be no violence, sex, car chases, or epiphanies in this film, we know a set-up when we hear one, so when those scenes arrive, we're enchanted. After carpeting the film with wall-to-wall voice-over, McKee rants, "And God help you, no narration!" Kaufman gets everything he wants by confessing to the contrivance.

Best of all, he gets laughs. *Adaptation* is hysterical. Kaufman may not be a Strindberg or Kafka, but unlike them, he balances his darkness with wit. And as everybody in show biz knows, when they're laughing, you're winning.

At times though, *Adaptation* still seems at risk of flying apart. For beneath its vivid surface are the agitations of ragged souls fighting to restore the balance of life. Images flit from story to story, in and out of suspicious realities. But Spike Jonze kept a firm grip on the pieces, so that, notwithstanding flashbacks and flutter cuts, the chronology and causality is clear and we have no problem telling a masturbation fantasy from fictional reality. The greater problem for the audience is sorting out when Kaufman is kidding and when he means it.

How seriously does Kaufman take any of this? I think he's always kidding, and therefore always serious. Kidding is his M.O. The final irony is that Kaufman goes crazy with a purpose. Somewhere at the back of his mind I sense a guy who knows exactly what he's doing, making it happen, smiling through, profoundly sane. Behind the eccentricity is someone, let's call him Charles K., who's ultimately in charge. Because without Charles K. *Adaptation* wouldn't be meaningful or comic. The only way to get laughs is to step back, eye the madness, and attack with wit. It takes a calm objectivity to see the foolishness, vanity, and absurdity in the world, society, and yourself for what they are and make us laugh at it all. I lift a glass to Charles K.

CAST AND CREW CREDITS

COLUMBIA PICTURES Presents
In Association with INTERMEDIA FILMS
A MAGNET/CLINICA ESTETICO Production

NICOLAS CAGE   MERYL STREEP   CHRIS COOPER

ADAPTATION

TILDA SWINTON   CARA SEYMOUR   BRIAN COX   JUDY GREER

MAGGIE GYLLENHAAL   RON LIVINGSTON   JAY TAVARE

Casting by	*Executive Producers*	*Costume Designer*	*Visual Effects Supervisor*
JUSTINE BADDELEY and KIM DAVIS-WAGNER	CHARLIE KAUFMAN PETER SARAF	CASEY STORM	GRAY MARSHALL
Music by	*Editor*	*Production Designer*	*Director of Photography*
CARTER BURWELL	ERIC ZUMBRUNNEN, A.C.E.	KK BARRETT	LANCE ACORD

Produced by
EDWARD SAXON VINCENT LANDAY JONATHAN DEMME

Based on the book "The Orchid Thief" by
SUSAN ORLEAN

Screenplay by
CHARLIE KAUFMAN and DONALD KAUFMAN

Directed by
SPIKE JONZE

CAST OF CHARACTERS
(in order of appearance)

Charlie Kaufman . . . . Nicolas Cage	Orlean Dinner Guests (cont'd) . . . . Paul Jasmin
Valerie . . . . Tilda Swinton	Lisa Love
Susan Orlean. . . . . Meryl Streep	Wendy Mogel
John Laroche . . . . Chris Cooper	David O. Russell
Matthew Osceola . . . . Jay Tavare	Alice the Waitress . . . . Judy Greer
Russell . . . . G. Paul Davis	Caroline . . . . Maggie Gyllenhaal
Randy. . . . . Roger Willie	David. . . . . Bob Stephenson
Ranger Tony. . . . . Jim Beaver	Charles Darwin . . . . Bob Yerkes
Donald Kaufman . . . . Nicolas Cage	Laroche's Dad. . . . . Lynn Court
Amelia . . . . Cara Seymour	Laroche's Uncle . . . . Roger E. Fanter
Augustus Margary. . . . . Doug Jones	Laroche's Mom . . . . Sandra Gimpel
Ranger Steve Neely . . . . Stephen Tobolowsky	Laroche's Wife . . . . Caron Colvett
Buster Baxley . . . . Gary Farmer	EMT . . . . Larry Krask
Defense Attorney . . . . Peter Jason	Marty. Ron Livingston
Prosecutor. . . . . Gregory Itzin	Robert McKee. . . . . Brian Cox
Orlean's Husband . . . . Curtis Hanson	McKee Lecture Attendee. . . . . John Etter
Orlean Dinner Guests . . . . Agnes Badoo	Police Officer . . . . Ray Berrios
Paul Fortune	Kaufman's Mother . . . . Nancy Lenehan

CREW

Stand-in for Mr. Cage . . . . Marco Kyris
Stand-in for Ms. Streep . . . . Julie Janney
Stand-in for Mr. Cooper. . . . . Jonathan Paley
Kaufman Twins . . . . Harris Mann
Marc Coppola

Stunt Coordinator . . . . Dan Bradley
Stunts . . . . Scott Rogers
Rick Barker
Chris Carnel
Lane Leavitt
Norbert Phillips
Darren Prescott
Eddie Yansick
Alligator Puppeteer . . . . Conor McCullagh

Unit Production Manager . . . . Karen Koch
First Assistant Director . . . . Thomas Patrick Smith
Second Assistant Director . . . . Brian O'Kelley

Ms. Streep's Clothing Designed by Ann Roth

Art Director . . . . Peter Andrus
Set Decorator. . . . . Gene Serdena

Script Supervisor . . . . Chiemi Karasawa
Camera Operator. . . . . Thomas H. Lohmann
First Assistant Camera . . . . Mark H. Williams
Jamie Felz
Second Assistant Camera . . . . Nina Chien
Steadicam Operator . . . . Paul Taylor
Camera Loader. . . . . Matthew W. Williams
Motion Control Operator. . . . . Joseph Stevenson
Video Assist . . . . Hans Michael Pickel
Wardrobe Supervisors . . . . Stacy M. Horn
Shari D. Gray
Costumers . . . . Anita Brown
Marina Marit
Deborah Travis
Makeup Department Head . . . . Joel Harlow
Makeup. . . . . Lynn Barber
Isabel Harkins
Allen Weisinger
Makeup and Hair for Ms. Streep . . . . J. Roy Helland

Hair Department Head . . . . Roz Music
Hair Stylists . . . . Joseph Coscia
Larry Waggoner
Chief Lighting Technician . . . . Mike Adler
Assistant Chief Lighting Technician. . . . . . . Chris Weigand
Key Grip . . . . Gino Nix

Second Grip . . . . Pie Griffiths
Dolly Grips . . . . Zoli Hajdu
Danny M. Anderson
Production Mixer . . . . Drew Kunin
Boom Operators . . . . Lawrence L. Commans
Mark W. Fay
Special Effects . . . . Gary D'Amico
Location Manager . . . . Rick Schuler
Assistant Location Managers . . . . Kent James Stewart Barber
Carson Turner
Production Supervisor . . . . Andrew J. Sacks
Production Coordinator. . . . . Rick C. Taplin
Assistant Production Coordinator . . . . Andrew Hayes
Production Secretary . . . . Andrew Ortner
Production Accountant . . . . Seve Spracklen
Assistant Production Accountant. . . . . Jonilyn Bissett
Construction Coordinator. . . . . Chris Forster
Construction Foreman . . . . Anders Rundblad
Lead Painter. . . . . Michael Leblovic
Paint Foreman. . . . . David Steiner
Labor Foreman . . . . Robert Davis
Lead Greens . . . . Porfirio Silva
Standby Greens . . . . Jess Anscott
Art Department Coordinator . . . . Patricia McNulty
Set Designers . . . . Lynn Christopher
Peter R. Davidson
Leadman. . . . . Grant D. Samson
Swing Gang . . . . Jamie Fleming
Bobby Pollard
On-Set Dresser . . . . Christian Kastner
Property Master . . . . Jeffrey Paul Johnson
Assistant Property Master . . . . Christopher Vail

Still Photographer . . . . Ben Kaller
2nd Second Assistant Director. . . . . Gregory J. Smith
Researcher . . . . Michelle Madden
Production Associates . . . . Krista Parris
Emma Wilcockson
Assistants to Spike & Vincenzo   Howard Shur
Jennifer Porst
Assistant to Mr. Cage. . . . . Stephen Bures
Assistant to Ms. Streep . . . . Emily Sklar
Production Assistants. . . . . Gary Bevans
Nathan Oliver
Krista Martin
Andy Lucskay
Joseph Patridge
Janette Kim
Michael G. Maurer

138

Casting Associate	Cate Engel
Extras Casting	Rich King / Kelly Hunt
Caterer	Hanna Brothers Catering
Craft Service	Kevin Pickett
Medic.	Michael R. Berry
Precision Driving.	Bondelli Precision Driving Team
Transportation Captain	Griff Ruggles
Transportation Co-Captain	Robby Stinton

Second Unit

2nd Unit Director.	Dan Bradley
First Assistant Director	Nick Satriano
Second Assistant Directors	Dave Riebel
	Matthew D. Smith
Director of Photography	James Fealy
Gaffer	Jim Frohna
Key Grip.	Joseph Messier
Production Supervisors	Maria K. Chavez
	Shoshana Horowitz

Sound Designer Richard Beggs

Additional Editing by.	Larry Law
1st Assistant Editor	Eric Osmond
Assistant Editor	Nathan FitzGerald
Supervising Sound Editor	Michael Kirchberger
Assistant Sound Editors.	Jeremy Molod
	Julia Shirar
Apprentice Sound Editor	Everett Moore
Dialogue Editors	David A. Cohen
	David Bergad
Sound Effects Editor	Peter Staubli
ADR Editor.	David Bach
Foley Supervisor	Bill Storkson
Foley Artist	Marnie Moore
Foley Mixer	Nick Peck
Foley Recordist.	Jory Prum
Re-recording Mixers.	Lora Hirschberg
	Kent Sparling
Re-recording Services by	Skywalker Sound
Loop Group	The Reel Team
Music Editor	Adam Milo Smalley
Assistant Music Editor	Bryan Lawson
Score Mixer.	Michael Farrow
Title Design by.	Geoff McFetridge
Titles by	Pacific Title
Digital Opticals by	Rods and Cones
Scanning and Recording by.	Riot Pictures
Color Timer	Bob Fredrickson
Negative Cutter	Mary Nelson-Fraser & Associates

Visual Effects by Gray Matter FX

Supervising Producer	Margaux Mackay
Digital Producer	Albert Mason
Compositors	Christine Petrov
	Dan Trezise
	David Crawford
	Michael Maloney
	Linda Henry
	Kristin Johnson
Rotoscope Artist	George Rowles
2D Artist	Paul Graff
Bee Sequence CG Character Animator	Beau Cameron
Bee Sequence Lighting Digital Artist	Kent Lidke
Bee Sequence Compositor	Joan Kim
Systems Administrator.	Eric Jordan
Accountant	Anzhey Barantsevich

Evolution Sequence by Digital Domain

Leslie Ekker

John Allardice	Richard Bjorlin
Cris Blyth	Shannan Burkley
Jodi Campanaro	Jean-Marc Demmer
Sean Devereaux	Nikos Kalaitzidis
Julien Meesters	Eileen O'Connor
Randy Sharp	Greg Teegarden
Ed Ulbrich	Vernon R. Wilbert, Jr.

Prosthetic Makeup for Mr. Cage
Kevin Yagher

Special Makeup Effects by Artist's Asylum

Makeup Effects Designer	Tony Gardner
Makeup Effects Producer.	Scott Malchus
Project Manager	Jessica Huebner
Lead Artist	David Smith
Effects Artists	Lilo Tauvao
	Vance Hartwell
Lead Mold-maker.	Paul Barnes
Effects Technician	Paul Salamoff

Soundtrack on Astralwerks

Columbia Pictures Industries, Inc., is the author of this film (motion picture) for the purpose of copyright and other laws.

Filmed at Warner Bros. Studios
Burbank, California
And on location in California, New York and Florida

ABOUT THE FILMMAKERS

Spike Jonze (Director) *Adaptation* is the second feature film directed by Spike Jonze, who made his debut with *Being John Malkovich*, which garnered four Academy Award® nominations.

Prior to *Being John Malkovich*, Jonze was best known as an award-winning music-video, short film, and commercial director. He got his start working as a photographer and co-directing (with Mark Gonzales) *Blind Video Days* (skate video).

His direction of the Beastie Boys' "Sabotage" music-video (1994), a spoof of 1970s television cop shows, received critical praise and numerous awards. Ever since, Jonze's music-videos have regularly been nominated for MTV Video Music Awards. He has worked with such talented artists as Bjork, The Pharcyde, Fatboy Slim, Daft Punk, R.E.M., Sean Lennon, and Weezer.

He produced *Human Nature*, based on an original script by Charlie Kaufman.

Charlie Kaufman (Screenplay By/Executive Producer) Charlie Kaufman previously collaborated with director Spike Jonze on *Being John Malkovich,* for which he received an Academy Award® nomination for Best Original Screenplay. Kaufman's next script was *Human Nature*, starring Tim Robbins, Patricia Arquette, and Rhys Ifans, directed by Michel Gondry and produced by Jonze. Kaufman wrote the screenplay for *Confessions of a Dangerous Mind*, directed by George Clooney. *Mind* is adapted from game-show host Chuck Barris' cult memoir about his days in the CIA. Most recently Kaufman was the screenwriter for *Eternal Sunshine of the Spotless Mind*, directed by Gondry, starring Jim Carrey and Kate Winslet.

Kaufman has also written for several television series, including "The Dana Carvey Show," "Get a Life," and "Ned and Stacey."

PRAISE FOR ADAPTATION

"A startlingly fresh look at the despair of an artist trying to be passionate about what he does in a bottom-line era….Together [Kaufman and his fictional brother Donald] embody the hilarious, desperate and very real tug of war between the art of screenwriting and the commerce of Hollywood." —PEN Center USA Judges, on awarding its 2003 Literary Award to Charlie Kaufman's screenplay *Adaptation*

"Following up on their existential black comedy *Being John Malkovich*, writer Charlie Kaufman and director Spike Jonze have one-upped themselves. Their new *Adaptation* journeys into the mind of a self-obsessed writer named Charlie Kaufman as he writes the movie we're watching. It's a Cubist-like fracturing of the real and reel worlds that artists from Pirandello to Magritte would have applauded. But the movie is no mere stunt. Kaufman and Jonze take huge risks to ponder the whole notion of passion—our desire as human beings for passion in our lives and the emptiness one feels when it is missing….

"Jonze's direction is graceful, deeply felt but surprisingly without self-consciousness. Ideas and images flow easily. The history of the world is distilled in a minute-long montage. Darwin puts in a brief appearance. And a writer questioning where he came from leads to a shot of a baby sliding from the birth canal.

"Wouldn't it be amusing if this highly original screenplay were to get nominated for best adaptation?" —Kirk Honeycutt, *Hollywood Reporter*

"Every bit as clever and surprising as *Malkovich*."
—Todd McCarthy, *Variety*

"One of the year's best." —Joel Siegel, *Good Morning America*

"Screenwriter Charlie Kaufman and director Spike Jonze (the inspired duo that made *Being John Malkovich*) have created a fun-undrum of a movie that's full of stories within stories, ideas within ideas, questions within questions and metaphors within metaphors.

"It's the cinematic equivalent of those Russian wooden dolls that pack neatly inside one another. You're invited to pull them out, one by one, spread them in any configuration you'd like, and decide what this movie is about."
 —Desson Howe, *The Washington Post*

"Charlie Kaufman is one of Hollywood's hottest It boys. At a time when so many movies seem formulaic—sequels, prequels and comic books— Kaufman's scripts are like the products of chaos theory."
 —Belinda Luscombe, *Time* magazine

"Smart, inventive, passionate and rip-roaringly funny...The most original and outrageous film comedy since [Kaufman and Jonze] first teamed on *Being John Malkovich*, in 1999....

"*Adaptation* is about obsession: for an orchid, for writing, for finding something or someone to obsess about. As Donald tells Charlie, 'You are what you love, not what loves you.' Few scripts toss more challenging balls in the air, and Jonze juggles them all with artful, light-stepping ease. It's magic."
 —Peter Travers, *Rolling Stone*

"*Adaptation* is fantastic, in every sense of the word."
 —Glenn Kenny, *Premiere*

"Moving and mind-bending."
 —Andrew Johnston, *US Weekly*

"Spry and inquisitive in spirit, *Adaptation*, like *Pulp Fiction*, at once humorously challenges and then reaffirms, tongue in cheek, the basic rules of cinematic storytelling, poking and prodding with unflagging fervor and intellectual curiosity the parameters that have been arbitrarily fobbed off on the art of film by the American Hollywood system. *Adaptation* is the sole major studio film so far of 2002 to challenge—narratively and structurally—the basic tenets of cinema, to push the envelope and challenge filmmakers and, make no mistake, audiences as well, to step up and attempt something more than the obvious. It's a twenty-first century pop angst commentary, and a uniquely American masterpiece."
—Brent Simon, *Entertainment Weekly*

"*Adaptation* is the best movie of the year."
—Andrew Sarris, *The New York Observer*

"This movie plays with time in the same way that *Being John Malkovich* played with corporeality. And once again Kaufman's collaborator is director Spike Jonze, who takes what could have been just riffs and makes them work to beguiling effect. He uses slow-motion nature photography, time-lapse sequences that begin billions of years before the invention of cameras, and at one point even cuts to Charles Darwin, working out his theory of evolution." —Bruce Newman, *Mercury News*

"*Adaptation* is another dazzling, idea-crammed, unconventional comedy by the writer-director team responsible for *Being John Malkovich*. Cerebral where *Malkovich* was surreal, *Adaptation* is equally funny and somehow more affecting." —Jonathan Foreman, *New York Post*

"The year's best film." —Mike D'Angelo, *Time Out New York*

"The multiple ways the film self-referentially doubles back on itself are difficult to describe on the page but immediately accessible and easy to enjoy on screen. Kaufman and director Jonze, in effect the writer's psychic twin, count on our movie-savvy minds to understand cinema's potential for subterfuge and effortlessly make the illusion/reality/illusion leaps that are the heart of the film's appeal.

"In a typical bit of business, the film's title turns out to have two parallel meanings. While in Hollywood adaptation is the process of turning a book into a film, in the plant world it refers to what *Orchid Thief* protagonist Laroche calls 'a profound process' whereby mutable orchids 'figure out how to thrive in the world'....

"Novelists putting themselves into novels à la Philip Roth is not new, and the idea of a film about a screenwriter making things up as he goes along is not unprecedented either. *Paris When It Sizzles*, written by George Axelrod and starring William Holden and Audrey Hepburn, did it in 1963, 1964, and that was based on an even earlier French film.

"None of that takes away from the liberating feeling of madcap originality that is *Adaptation*'s strength. Though Kaufman's script gently mocks the notion that writing should have something different as its goal, that is what's been accomplished here.

"There may be, as Orlean's book informs us, 30,000 varieties of orchids in the world, but in the universe of film there's never been an adaptation quite like the one we have here."

—Kenneth Turan, *Los Angeles Times*

"Along with *Barton Fink*, this is probably the best depiction of writer's block on film."   —Jami Bernard, *New York Daily News*

"Brilliant! Wildly original and deeply entertaining. *Adaptation* is one of the best films of the year."   —Paul Clinton, CNN

"Like no movie before it, *Adaptation* risks everything—its cool, its credibility, its very soul—to expose the horror of making art for the business of entertainment. By the time it's all over, you might even recognize what Kaufman, Jonze, and Cage have accomplished as an old-fashioned triumph of the human spirit. Of course, to get there, the movie has to pull itself through a postmodern, self-reflexive swamp. (And a real swamp, too.)

"This is epic, funny, tragic, demanding, strange, original, boldly sincere filmmaking. And the climax—the portion that either sinks the entire movie or self-critically explains how so many others derail—is bananas.

"It's possible to argue that what the finale amounts to is fraud. But really it's the extraordinary act of a film and its makers chewing off their leg to set themselves free. That's ludicrous and desperate and savage. But it's also revolutionary—and highly evolved." —*The Boston Globe*

"It's official: The bar of cinema has been raised."

—Jauretsi Saizarbitoria, *Jane Magazine*

"What a bewilderingly brilliant and entertaining movie this is—a confounding story about orchid thieves and screenwriters, elegant New Yorkers and scruffy swamp rats, truth and fiction. *Adaptation* is a movie that leaves you breathless with curiosity, as it teases itself with the directions it might take. To watch the film is to be actively involved in the challenge of its creation....

"I sat up during this movie. I leaned forward. I was completely engaged. It toyed with me, tricked me, played straight with me, then tricked me about that. Its characters are colorful because they care so intensely; they are more interested in their obsessions than they are in the movie, if you see what I mean. And all the time, uncoiling beneath the surface of the film, is the audacious surprise of the last 20 minutes, in which—well, to say the movie's ending works on more than one level is not to simply say it works on only two."—Roger Ebert, *Chicago Sun-Times*

"*Adaptation* is brain... ...week

"'*Do I have an original thought in m...*
    —Screenwriter...

"Yes, dear Charlie, yes...
who most need to ask th...
originality in spades with yc...
back at it again here. A comic...
pulls off a feat I would have thoug...
to dramatize the art and sullen craft c...
the schizoid head of virtually every wor...
pen or powered on a computer. That the h...
Kaufman himself leads me to the next astonish...
be a self-indulgent, head-up-its-*derrière* exercise, a...
anyone beyond his fellow legion of scribblers. But it...
    —Rick Groen,

"Who knew that a movie about not being able to write a movie
so . . . cinematic? One of *Adaptation*'s most astonishing features is tha...
Charlie labors over scenes which to the ear sound pretentious or shallow,
yet to the eye are accessible and profound.

"Kaufman and Jonze take the familiar and make it unfamiliar, whether
it is a narrative device, a stereotypical character, or an evolutionary theory.
Here they give us a curious array of hardy types—the smartypants New
York journalist, the solipsistic Hollywood screenwriter, and the self-taught
Florida redneck. Not all will survive their encounter.

"No conventional comedy asks whether it's survival of the fittest or
fate that's responsible for the species' perpetuation. *Adaptation* does.
Unconventionally it suggests that both the Hollywood formula film and
the Hollywood idea of romantic love may both be products of natural
selection."
    —Carrie Rickey, Philly.com